HOPE LIVES HERE

HOPE
LIVES
HERE

JANINE MAXWELL

HOPE LIVES HERE
Copyright © 2021 Janine Maxwell

Printed in China

Published by Giving Publishing, 2555 Northwinds Parkway, Alpharetta, GA 30009. In association with the literary agency of The WTA Group, Franklin, TN.

Published by iDisciple Publishing, 2555 Northwinds Parkway, Alpharetta GA 30009.

ISBN: 979-8-743-64898-6
Written by Janine Maxwell
Photography by Ian Maxwell.
Cover and layout design by Maggie Lian.

For information contact: www.heartforafrica.org

Endorsements

I read this through both tears and smiles. It stirred my hope, challenged my own indifference and, if I'm honest, I shook my head a few times and said, "Wow." We talk a lot about what Jesus would do if He were here. I think He'd be doing this. This is Jesus with skin. This is what the Kingdom of Heaven is, does and looks like. Here and now. If you say you love Jesus, you should probably read this.

Charles Martin
New York Times Bestselling Author

Hunger, poverty, and disease are colorblind. Janine Maxwell's HOPE LIVES HERE is the inspiring story of how she and her family leveraged their privilege to offer real promise to children, a community, and a country a world away. This is a must-read story of what ordinary people can do when they wield extraordinary compassion, respect, and love in the service of others.

Laura Lane
Chief Corporate Affairs, Communications and Sustainability Officer, UPS

For the past 15 years, Andy and I have had the privilege of watching Janine and Ian Maxwell take the deepest dive of obedience to God we've ever seen. And we've watched God respond by doing things only He can do. Under the Maxwells' leadership, Heart for Africa has grown into a thriving, successful organization focused on fighting hunger, caring for orphans, decreasing poverty, and providing education in the tiny kingdom of Eswatini. We've had the privilege of experiencing firsthand the critical need for this ministry's mission. Heart for Africa is an important partner in North Point Ministries' efforts to share the love of Christ throughout the world. Janine's relentless pursuit to rescue children abandoned in the most extreme circumstances, along with her and Ian's shared vision to develop sustainability at Project Canaan should serve as a model for organizations across the globe. the service of others.

HOPE LIVES HERE is not just the title of her third book; it is the insistent, immutable drumbeat of daily life at Project Canaan.

Sandra and Andy Stanley
North Point Ministries

This is the book I've been waiting for! Telling people about Project Canaan and Heart for Africa can be overwhelming because of the scope of the vision, the care and research that goes into each decision, and how tirelessly they work toward sustainability and raising the next generation of leadership in Eswatini. Janine does an incredible job of bringing all of the pieces together in a way that is easy to understand, while still encompassing the massive vision given to her and Ian. My family and I first went to Eswatini in 2008 on a service trip with Heart for Africa. Since then, I have watched the organization grow and evolve. In August

2021 I will be marrying Spencer and officially joining the Maxwell family!

Jane Balasz *(Soon to be Maxwell)*

There is no one like Janine Maxwell. HOPE LIVES HERE is a gripping chronicle of her journey to bring Heart for Africa's mission of HOPE to life. The book describes the inconceivable challenges and difficulties that Heart for Africa has overcome to bring stability to Project Canaan, while also building bridges that will carry this incredible community into the future. Janine's devotion and compassion shine through on every page and it is clear that HOPE has paved a road of progress. This is why we are proud to support Heart for Africa through a partnership that brings the life-saving nutrition and high-quality protein of the humble egg to communities in rural Eswatini.

Tim Lambert
Chief Executive Officer, Egg Farmers of Canada
President, World Egg Organisation

Feed My Starving Children has had the privilege of partnering with Heart for Africa/Project Canaan since 2009. During that time, we have seen Janine and Ian's love in action becoming the guardians for hundreds of children and feeding hundreds of thousands of children in Eswatini. Janine and Ian show Christ's love every day through their

HOPE initiative. We are honored to work with this couple whose love for Jesus and the people of Eswatini is relentless.

Mark Crea
Executive Director/CEO
Feed My Starving Children

HOPE LIVES HERE is a book that will encourage the world during a time when we all need to find hope in something greater than ourselves. Taiwan is proud to partner with the Kingdom of Eswatini and we are encouraged that students from Changhua Senior High School are actively involved in supporting the work of Heart for Africa in Eswatini. Our commitment to helping provide water during a time of drought is only a small part of our commitment to the Kingdom. As a nation, we are thankful for the work that is being done at Project Canaan to save orphaned and abandoned children while providing employment for adults and bringing hope to a nation and to the world.

William Lai Ching-te
Vice President of Taiwan

When I first met Janine and heard about Heart for Africa, it was quickly quite obvious that here was a remarkable woman. The extent of this remarkability I truly discovered, though, when reading HOPE LIVES HERE, the book you probably have in your hand right now! While it reads like a crime novel page-turner, at the same time it also packs an emotional punch to a degree that I had to put it down on more than one occasion with tears in my eyes. Moreover and maybe most importantly, HOPE LIVES HERE gives valid and credible suggestions and examples on how to create positive change in developing countries like Eswatini and throughout Africa. Well done. It has been – and still is – a pleasure to work with Ian and Janine and the Heart for Africa team.

We at hummel, as in other Thornico companies, have worked with a multitude of NGO's in Africa through the last 20 years as part of our Company Karma philosophy, and the Heart of Africa charity ranks at the top amongst the most dedicated and professional that we have worked with to date. A pleasure!

Christian Nicholas Stadil
CEO and Owner
Thornico Group of companies, Denmark
(Here under the sportswear brand hummel)

God wants our availability, not our ability. Janine and Ian Maxwell's faith journey into the Heart for Africa is an inspiring story of what's possible when we trust the Lord's calling. The Maxwells dropped everything, including a successful marketing company in Canada, and moved to Swaziland (Eswatini) to provide a loving home for hundreds of orphans, the least of these, one child at a time. Their faith-walk led them to start Project Canaan with the first child, Joshua. Hope is alive and hope lives at Project Canaan. The story continues and reading the book will break your heart and give you hope through the love of Christ demonstrated through the Maxwells.

Steve Stirling
President and CEO
Map International

HOPE LIVES HERE is the remarkable and unlikely story of how Janine and Ian Maxwell bring hope to the tiny country of Eswatini in southern Africa. Herself adopted as an infant, Janine knows the power of a good home infused with faith. She and her husband bring profound compassion and untiring devotion to the task of caring for 300+ orphans and serving the community around Project Canaan. Their intentional goal is nothing less than creating future leaders for a country where tradition and hopelessness reinforce each other. Heartrending stories of abandoned babies they so happily welcome to their home speak vividly of how life and death are the closest neighbors when hopelessness prevails. Perhaps the most inspiring book I've read, it will remind you that there is good in the world, and that there is more good yet to be done.

Calvin W. Edwards
Founder & CEO, Calvin Edwards & Company

Contents

Dedication

This book is dedicated to my incredible family, who has supported this calling to serve "the least of these" in Africa with all their hearts and at a great personal sacrifice.

To my husband Ian: You are a man of integrity, who shows compassion and fairness through your patience, work ethic, and attention to detail. There is no one with whom I would rather be called to this ministry (aka *our wild ride*) other than you. You are my rudder and your leadership is an example of what a godly man and father are to all of our children.

To Spencer and Chloe: Thank you for being such good kids while being dragged all over Africa for your entire summer breaks for most of your childhood and for not giving up on us when we decided to move to Africa. You have become remarkable young adults who are already changing the world around you. Thank you for sharing your parents with hundreds of little ones who really needed a family and for loving them all unconditionally. Your support and commitment to our ever-growing family is a testament to God's faithfulness in your lives and your selflessness is an example for all to follow. May the Lord bless you and keep you, and continue to guide you in every step you take.

With love,
Janine/Mom

xoxoxo

Acknowledgments

I never wanted to write my first or second book—and really really didn't want to write this one. It's too hard, too personal, and too gut-wrenching to re-live many events, but I am thankful for all the people who continually pushed me to write this account of how Project Canaan came into existence and all that God has done in a short time.

I want to thank my high school English teacher, "Miss Hamilton" (now Mrs. Gayle Gill), for encouraging me in my love of words, storytelling, and writing. It was such a gift to have you be the first person to read this manuscript and encourage me to keep going, even as you were battling—and winning—your fight with cancer.

Thank you to my editor and friend, Cheryl Lewis, who worked tirelessly to make sure my stories flowed, didn't repeat, and were clear for the reader. Fixing my punctuation and Oxford commas was a full-time job on this book. Thank you for reading the manuscript over and over and over again and for lovingly helping me navigate my own emotions and hang-ups. Special thanks for pushing me to write about some of the betrayals we have experienced and for helping me to keep it real (not that the rest of the book isn't real enough). Sharing deep personal hurt is hard to do and feels like airing dirty laundry, but it is what it is and I am thankful for you helping me across that river of sadness.

Pete and Julie Wilkerson, what can I say? You have been our dearest and most trusted friends. Thank you for opening your home to us every time we are in the U.S. and for letting us fill your front porch and spare bedroom with Amazon packages. Thank you for laughing with us until we cry and crying with us until we laugh. Thank you for doing anything and everything we ask, as crazy as some requests might be. You guys are simply the best and we are so thankful that the Lord brought you into our lives in 2007.

David Bryant, you have become so much more than our Chief Development Officer; you have become a friend I can trust with my hopes, dreams, and frustrations. You are a shoulder to cry upon and a high-five when we celebrate. Thank you for reading the early manuscript and for encouraging me to get it done! I love working with you and serving the Lord alongside you.

Thank you to my best friend, Jeanette Reed, who has helped me grow daily in my faith and who challenges me to draw closer to the Lord each and every day. You taught me to "ask Him" not you and what to do in any given circumstance. "What did the Lord say?" you respond to ALL of my questions. I just wanted to know what you thought, but you were always insistent that your opinion didn't matter. You were right and over the years you have retrained me to ask Him first (and then maybe you). I love you, friend, and can't imagine my life without you in it.

Thank you to my dear friend, Tricia Ford, who has walked side by side with us on this journey from the very first day. You were always there to pick me up and dust me off or hand me a tissue. Thank you for being a second mom to Spencer and Chloe when we moved to Africa and answering those challenging middle-of-the-night calls when their phone plan wouldn't dial internationally. I loved working with you for 14 years and miss you every day.

The work we are doing here is hard and complicated, but it is nothing compared to what the Deputy Prime Minister, Themba Masuku, and his team of dedicated Social Welfare officers deal with every day. Thank you for your courage, your tenacity, and your commitment to the children, the elderly, and the disabled people of Eswatini. While Jesus is their only hope, you are the hands and feet of Jesus every day. Please don't give up. The nation needs you to stay strong and courageous.

Being a medical professional in Eswatini is a challenge on the best days and devastating on the worst. From the very beginning, Dr. Richard and Dr. Moira Lemmer have supported our dream to provide excellent medical care for our children and our staff and we couldn't have done it without them. You provide the backbone to our medical clinic and medical care on Project Canaan and we appreciate you.

I'm grateful to my friends and teachers, Dr. Pawelos, Dr. Mukemba, Dr. Dlamini, Dr. Mafulu, and Dr. Kunene for being patient while giving me a deep education on pediatric HIV/AIDS, tuberculosis, meningitis, malnutrition, and all other pediatric health issues. Thank you for holding my hand, wiping my tears, and watching the hand of God at work.

Thank you to Cynthia Horton-Xaba for reading the manuscript and making sure I didn't offend my Swazi friends and family or go to jail for being too bold. Thank you, Gcebile Shongwe-Dlamini and Khosi Mamba, for being my teachers of all things Swazi and for your grace in helping me understand or dig deeper into the unknown.

My appreciation goes to Janet and Jere Scott for all that they have done for the ministry and us personally since we first met in 2005. You have served with us across the continent of Africa, praying, laughing, and crying with us. You have built buildings, put out fires, and cooked great meals. You love well, pray well and I don't know any others who are 80+ that serve the way you do—with all of your heart, body, and soul. We only hope that we can continue to serve like you as we (swiftly) approach our golden years.

We are grateful for Jerry and Jean Eickhoff, a couple who have had such an impact on my life. I met Jerry in Tunisia (of all places) at a North Point Community Church partner conference. It was there that we became fast friends and you and Jean have been a never-ending source of encouragement, love, prayers, and connections to other people who want to help. Thank you for always being there when I need you and even when I don't know that I need you!

Thank you to the people who have sacrificed so much to come and live in Africa to serve "the least of these" as long-term volunteers. We are blessed to have served with you, whether it was for one year or for many. Knowing that we have your support and can trust you is critical to our mental health. Thank you also to the thousands of people who have come on an 11-day trip to help support us in that way. Your visits are encouraging and help us know that we are loved from afar.

I wish I could list all of the people who have given generously and sacrificially to help support this ministry, but some of you wouldn't want to be publicly acknowledged and it would fill too many pages. Without your financial support, we would not be able to feed children, care for orphans, employ people or educate the future leaders of this nation. We extend a special note of thanks to those who've stepped up to become Khutsala Artisans ambassadors and angels in our Christmas ornament fundraising program. The joy you spread is invaluable!

Who would've known that the teenager I met in 2006 and traveled to Africa with many times would then end up traveling with me (with Spencer Maxwell and Rachel Smoltz) in 2008 for the International Youth Conference in Taiwan—and then end up working in the marketing department at Heart for Africa? Maggie Taylor Lian, you are precious to us! I love that you're the one who has designed my front and back cover and laid out this entire book. God sure knew what He was doing when He crossed our paths and definitely picked the very best person for the job. Thank you, Maggie, for always listening for His voice, recognizing the sound of it, and being obedient to it. It is a joy serving with you.

I would not be who I am today without the love and support of my mom and dad, Bernice and Russ Willis. They taught me to be truthful in all things, mindful of the people around me, and generous with my money. My mother reminded me often that all we have comes from HIM, so don't be afraid to give back to Him, that which is His. I miss my parents every day and know they would LOVE Project Canaan and all of their many grandchildren.

Most of all, I know I dedicated this book to my husband and children, but I want to say once more to Ian, Spencer, and Chloe Maxwell, you are the BEST and I love you! Thank you for believing in me and pursuing God's plan for your lives. Seeking, listening, and honoring His design is always the right way to go. Countless lives are changed because of it!

A land map of Project Canaan

A Front Entrance

B El Rofi Medical Clinic

C Kufundza Center

D Khutsala Artisans

E Chapel

F Welcome Center

G Living Water Dam

H Imphilo Amphitheater

I Project Canaan Academy

J Children's Campuses

K The Lodge

L Maxwell Home

M Thornico Field

N Greenhouse

O Lusito Mechanic Shop

P Dairy

Q Layer Barns

R Pipeline

Visit our website to learn more about Project Canaan:

www.HeartforAfrica.org

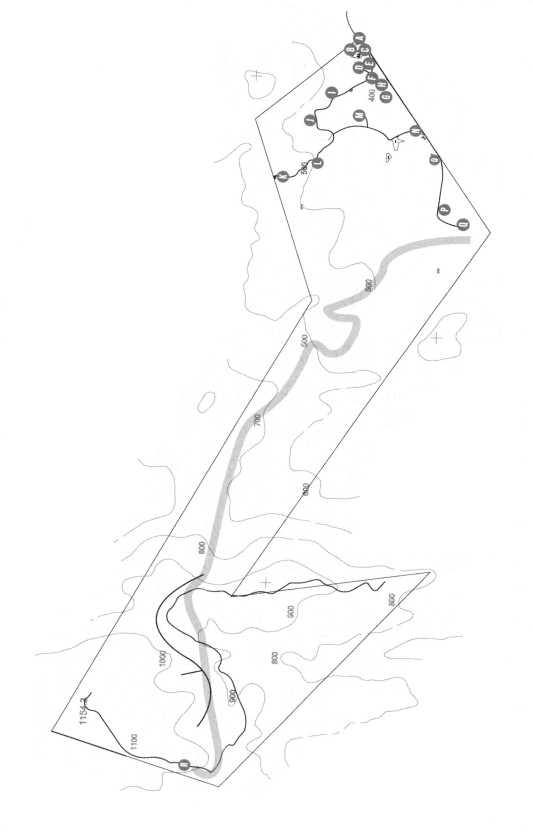

Project Canaan Timeline | 2009-2029

2009
- purchased land
- cleared land and planted first crop

2010 — **Hunger**
- 1st harvest of maize
- chapel is built and dedicated

2012 — **Orphans** ———————— CHILD COUNT: 22
- El Roi baby home - lower campus opens
- Maxwell's move to Eswatini

2013 — **Poverty** ———————— CHILD COUNT: 46
- Khutsala Artisans opens
- dairy operation begins

2014 — **Education** ———————— CHILD COUNT: 84
- Project Canaan Academy preschool opens
- Living Water dam is built

2015 ———————— CHILD COUNT: 105
- children's middle campus opens

2016 ———————— CHILD COUNT: 146
- aquaponics system started
- layer barns receive their first flocks
- drought begins

2018 ———————— CHILD COUNT: 216
- water security achieve with water from the mountain

2019 ———————— CHILD COUNT: 257
- 10th Anniversary celebration
- agricultural restart
- fires

2020 ———————— CHILD COUNT: 275
- global Coronavirus pandemic
- all travel and visitors suspended

2021 ———————— ESTIMATED CHILD COUNT: 308
- Special Needs home for children opens
- children's upper campus opens

2023 ———————— ESTIMATED CHILD COUNT: 371
- Project Canaan Academy middle school opens

2025 ———————— ESTIMATED CHILD COUNT: 433
- Project Canaan Academy high school opens

2026 ———————— ESTIMATED CHILD COUNT: 464
- The Bridge Program launches

2029 ———————— ESTIMATED CHILD COUNT: 558
- Project Canaan Academy 1st high school graduation!

2030 ———————— ESTIMATED CHILD COUNT: 590

The Bridge is open

HOPE
LIVES
HERE

INTRODUCTION
How It All Started

If you've not yet read one or both of my previous books, *It's Not Okay With Me* and *Is It Okay With You?*, let me summarize the portions of my life they covered. I will make this short and sweet so that we can move on to the real meat of the story: *Project Canaan*, A Place of HOPE in the tiny Kingdom of Eswatini (formerly known as Swaziland), Africa—the place we now call home.

I grew up in the small town of Matheson in Northern Ontario, Canada. The population of the town and surrounding communities was 3,500+. We had snow from early October and the ice on the lakes broke around the May 24 weekend (also known as Queen Victoria's birthday and the May "24-pack" weekend). While I enjoyed a safe and carefree childhood, I don't miss the cold and snow at all.

My parents, Bernice and Russell Willis, were pharmacists who, after graduating from the University of Toronto, migrated north to avoid the pollen in southern Ontario that triggered my father's asthma. Somewhere along the way, they discovered that they were not able to get pregnant; after registering with the Children's Aid Society, they awaited the arrival of a baby boy. Receiving a call that there was a baby girl available changed their plans and they jumped at the chance to welcome me into their family.

I always knew I was adopted and my parents made it particularly clear that I had been chosen. Truth be told, until I was a teenager, I believed that my parents had gone into a grocery-type store where they found produce-department-style shelving lined with newborn babies. In my version, they had slowly walked past the babies cooing and smiling on the shelf until they saw me—obviously the cutest baby of them all—and that is how they chose me and took me home. I couldn't visualize the checkout process of the store, but that didn't deter me from owning the fact that I had been chosen and I was theirs.

(I didn't realize how important this perception of how I came to the Willis family would be until recently when the children we are raising in Eswatini started asking where they came from and who was their "real mom." Much more on this later.)

My high school days in Northern Ontario were rough. I was bored. I talked back to my (very strict) parents a lot and that landed me in a private boarding school called Grenville Christian College (GCC) in Brockville, Ontario. There has been a lot of controversy about GCC over the years, with some calling it a cult, prison, or wonderful place of education. It was eventually closed due to the controversy and my opinion of the school shall remain private. What I will tell you is that I met my husband, Ian, there. He was in 10th grade and I was in 12th grade when we were put in Mr. and Mrs. Childs' Saturday night family and became fast friends. It would be many years after graduating from high school and university that our friendship grew into love and then marriage.

From high school, I moved to Springfield, Missouri to attend Evangel College (now Evangel University). I loved my time in the Midwest with my Canadian friends, the Mainse kids. I graduated in 1985 and headed north with the burning desire to live in Toronto, which I thought was the coolest city in the world (and it was!). I begged my way into a promotional marketing job, which paid a $200/week draw against commission, and, after a couple of years, I decided to start my marketing agency. After all, how hard could it be for a 24-year-old woman with no marketing or business degree to start her own shop? One uncle told me that I would never succeed because only the best could win in that industry, and my dad suggested that I wasn't really an entrepreneur, but just unemployed when I quit my job to start my business. Ten years later, ONYX Marketing Group was one of the largest marketing agencies in Canada.

On September 11, 2001, I was in New York City at a "Marketing to Kids" conference with a co-worker and clients from Kellogg's when the first plane hit the World Trade Center. We ran up to our rooms to watch the news and then quickly dashed back to the lobby to await further instruction. That came by way of police gunfire on the street with an evacuation notice that there may be explosives in Grand Central Station, which was right below our lobby. Ian was on a flight to Chicago from Toronto at the time and, when the flight landed, he learned what was happening in NYC; he knew that I was there. There was nothing we could do, with no way to communicate, and our world flipped upside down.

It took us three days to get back to our children in Canada. When I arrived home, I was a puddle of tears, a ball of anxious nerves, and changed forever. I slid into depression and questioned everything—from why I was born to the meaning of life—and began a quest to find the answers to both questions. That journey led me to Africa in April 2003. My first visit was the catalyst for the title of my first book, *It's Not Okay with Me*, as I came face to face with abject poverty, children living on the street, child rape, babies dumped in the forest or river, young girls having sex for a loaf of bread, and the decimation of a generation of Africans by HIV/AIDS.

When I closed my eyes at night, I was haunted by the voices of the children I'd met and short life stories I had heard. I could see the emptiness in their eyes that matched the emptiness in their souls. I could still smell the odor of human waste, tiny bodies that hadn't been washed in years, fungus growing in their hair, and the rotting flesh of Kaposi Sarcoma that comes with advanced AIDS. I couldn't run away from it and there was nothing I could really do when I kept going back to Africa to "help." Raising money was the only real way I could help and so I started doing that.

I was completely distracted by my passion for the children of Africa and wanted nothing to do with the luxuries of my life. I couldn't focus at work; I stopped caring about petty things that used to bother me or fun things I once enjoyed. Going out for an expensive meal became stressful, because of the extravagance. I resented driving a new BMW SUV, so I turned in my leased vehicle and started driving the Le Sabre my dad could no longer drive.

I decided to sell my business so that I could work on helping the suffering children full time. How or what I was going to do was a mystery, but I just knew that Africa was my destiny. As I started to ponder and talk to potential buyers, I realized that I would have to do a "work-out" period of two to three years to properly transition my clients to their new agency home. I just didn't feel I had that much time. I couldn't sell the business;

I would have to just close it.

In 2005, it was estimated that there were 15 million children orphaned by HIV/AIDS in sub-Saharan Africa and it was further estimated there would be 40 million by the year 2010. I felt urgency like I had never felt urgency — I still feel that to this day.

In July 2004, we closed ONYX Marketing Group forever and started to pray about what would come next. On February 1, 2006, we launched *Heart for Africa*. By October 2006, we had moved to the United States to live in Alpharetta, Georgia; that would be home to our family and the organization for the seven years that followed. All of the details of this crazy adventure are chronicled in my first and second books.

The next three years saw us coming alongside many orphanages in multiple countries in Africa, and while we loved serving alongside the leadership of those homes and being a part of the children's lives, we struggled with not being able to do enough and/or not being able to do things the way we wanted to do them. We were simply outside support to the people doing the daily heavy lifting with the children who needed a special kind of love.

We wanted to do more.

One day, Ian had the vision to buy a piece of land that we could work ourselves. Chapter 13 in *Is It Okay With YOU?* tells the dramatic events that led up to meeting a man who gave us a personal check for $1 million to buy 2,500 acres of *African bush* in Swaziland.

In 2009, we took possession of the land that we now call Project Canaan.

There were no roads, no river or water, no electricity, no buildings, no fields—*nothing* but African bush.

And the journey began.

In 2012, the Maxwell family packed up their belongings and shipped them to Africa to start a new work, expand our family, and disciple a community.

This is where the story continues.

As with my other books, I have changed some of the names of the people involved to protect their identities and maintain their confidence. The stories and events I share are told to the very best of my knowledge and memory of said events. I use both the new and old names of the Kingdom of Swaziland and Eswatini, based upon the period the story takes place. As a point of clarity, *Heart for Africa* is a registered charity in the U.S., Canada, and Eswatini. Project Canaan is the land development project in Eswatini that is funded by the *Heart for Africa* charities.

CHAPTER ONE

Project Canaan: A Place of Hope

It was a very dark night and she was afraid. Labor had started earlier than she had expected, but she knew it was happening. This was her second child; her first had arrived when she was only 15 years old and the memory of that fear and pain still haunted her. She made her way to the pit latrine (outdoor toilet) that the family had used for many years and sat down on the old platform. The urgency grew and she pushed. This second child wasn't any easier than the first, but at least she knew what to expect. She pushed again until finally, the baby's head erupted from her tender teenage private area; soon the infant slipped on through into the pile of human waste below.

She was not quite sure how it happened, but the placenta followed and there was silence. She tried to see her newborn, but as she peered down there was no end to the darkness. It was as if the baby had been swallowed by the blackness itself. She cleaned herself up as best she could and made her way back to her stick-and-mud house.

She lay on her bed and urged herself to go back to sleep, but sleep would not come. Five hours later, the sun started to peek up above the mountain range in the distance and she crept back to the pit latrine to make sure the baby was dead.

To her shock, she heard a cry.

"Oh no," she thought, horrified. *"This can't be happening! The baby can't possibly still be alive after being there for five hours! Surely the newborn would have suffocated by now."*

Other family members were starting to stir, so she quickly ran and got a shovel. Frantically she scooped up some hot coals from the fire built to heat the leftover mealie meal (cooked maize) from the night before; it would make soft porridge for her and her 2-year-old daughter if there was enough to scrape from the side of the pot. She stumbled back to the pit latrine and flung the hot coals down onto the tiny newborn, whose cries were getting louder. Suddenly she heard footsteps coming toward her and she panicked. Who could it be? Would they hear the baby's cries? Would the baby be dead before the person opened the door? Would she be able to lie her way out of this disaster?

The door swung open and her uncle was looking directly into her soul. What had she done?! What was that noise coming from the depths of human waste? He held his breath and peered down into the toilet as she fell to the ground and sobbed.

What HAD she done?

Her uncle grabbed the shovel out of her hand and quickly filled it with sand, then dumped it atop the burning coals to put them out. He got another scoop and threw more in, then another until he could no longer see any of the glowing orange and yellow embers.

The family was awakened, the police were called and time stood still while they waited for help to arrive. Eventually, a truck with police officers arrived on the scene, but no one knew what to expect when they entered the crime scene. They tied a piece of rope around the young teenager's waist and lowered her, sobbing, down into the pit latrine to retrieve the body of her newborn baby. Her feet touched the stinking pile first and then it slowly climbed up her legs until she was thigh-deep in fresh sand, burnt, coals and hell. She found the baby and heard the whimpers coming from the tiny creature that looked like coal in the darkness. The police started to pull her up by her waist. She made it back through the hole and gasped for fresh air.

They swiftly wiped off the infant to discover it was a baby girl. She was badly burned—and she was alive. They rushed her to the hospital where she stayed, along with her teen mother, who had attempted the murder but was responsible for her care the next six weeks. It's customary there for a parent or adult to stay at the hospital with a sick child because there is not enough nursing staff to provide care for the child beyond medication and medical care.

The infant's face had melted and she'd lost part of her nose; her arms, hands, legs, and feet were burned. The medical staff did the best they could in a government hospital in a developing nation with minimal access to painkillers (nothing stronger than Tylenol or aspirin). Miraculously she lived! Six weeks later, they discharged the newborn and sent the mother and baby to the Mawelawela Woman's Prison.

The story you have just read probably sounds similar to some of the stories I shared in my first two books. Indeed, if you read them, you might think this book is just more of the same, but I promise you it's not.

After my first few trips to Africa, I felt I had to write *It's Not Okay With Me* so that the stories I had been told by children who had suffered unthinkable pain wouldn't be forgotten. They poured their hearts out to me and I wrote their stories so that even after death, they would not be forgotten; their suffering would be known and it would not be in vain. I felt as though I was writing each word with blood that had been spilled from their tiny bodies; my never-ending flow of tears soaked each page. My second book, *Is It Okay With You?* was my attempt to chronicle how we tried, as an organization (and family), to feed the hungry, rescue the orphans, help the poor, and educate the uneducated; but it was so difficult and most days seemed impossible. We worked diligently to come alongside other ministries all over Africa to help them work toward sustainability, but it was so hard. I could write two more books just about the episodes where we were robbed, taken advantage of, lied to, cheated, and hurt deeply by the people that we loved. While I won't brush those experiences under the rug, because it's part of the obstacles we face, I will focus more on many happier ones.

As we continued to serve in Africa, we knew that we couldn't "fix" things, nor was it our place to try to fix a place that wasn't our home, but we also had a moral and fiscally responsible compass that forced us to draw some very hard lines in the sand. There was a school in Kenya with a head teacher who insisted she had the right to strip students naked at the front of the class and beat them to make them pay attention better. We disagreed with her approach and, after a year of trying to disciple the head teacher and advocate for the children, we threw in the towel. It was not our home and not our school. We were just helping to fund it, so we stopped. Many people thought we were unreasonable and harsh, but our compass would not allow us to continue in that direction.

This book is different from the others. It chronicles a journey that is most definitely "a road less traveled," but one that will share the joy that came from sadness, the hope that came from hopelessness, and the healing that came from pain.

In 2008, after two years of key learnings (aka endless frustrations) of how and how not to work in developing nations, the Lord gave Ian a vision and it was radical. Rather than coming alongside other children's homes and farms, the Lord showed Ian a 2,500-acre piece of land and told him to buy it. The ticket price on the land was $1 million in 2008. (References to money are U.S. dollars unless otherwise noted.)

For those of you who don't think God still speaks, please read this story carefully. I may not convince you, but let's give it a go.

Ian wasn't one of those guys who would ever say, "God told me this," or "God said that." Ian wasn't a man who had a lot of desire to step out of his comfortable box into the unknown, especially not the unknown of buying land in a tiny kingdom in Africa run by the last absolute monarch on the continent. Ian is an economist, not a risk-taker, and so when I tell you that God spoke to him, I mean it. In fact, when Ian first started telling me about the land, I thought he was crazy and refused to drive out and even see the property! I am a practical get-it-done gal and it seemed to me I was busy getting things done while he was "daydreaming" about buying land in Africa.

I remember asking him what he would do with 2,500 acres of land and his eyes lit up and twinkled with excitement. One time he told me that he envisioned having dairy cows on the land, so we could provide milk to children and sell locally. My reply was to remind him that he had never seen a cow in person (city boy to his roots). He went on to say we would grow vegetables to eat, feed children in need, and sell to generate income. I, being the ever-supportive wife, reminded him that he doesn't even eat vegetables! He would talk about the many children who would call this land home and he could see hundreds of people working on the land, finally able to provide for their families.

He was crazy!

At one point I wondered if this was his beginning of a mid-life crisis and considered suggesting that he buy a little red sports car, but he was serious. In truth, he had never been so serious about anything in his life. I told him that I would pray about this crazy vision, but the Lord would have to skywrite for me to buy into the plan. We had not told our board or staff about this idea of buying land because, at that time, we were just struggling to make payroll at *Heart for Africa*. Did I mention that the seller of the land was asking $1 million?

After a long summer serving in Africa, we returned to Georgia and were invited to a meeting where we met a wealthy man who had heard about us and dropped into our meeting unexpectedly. Halfway through our time of sharing, he started to describe a vision that the Lord had given him. He told us of rolling hills and fields filled with vegetables. There were a dairy, vocational training, and lots of children who needed homes. I started to cry. Ian looked at me and then looked back at the man and told him about the land in Africa. The man paused, the room froze and I tried to hold myself together (unsuccessfully, by the way) as he asked Ian how much the land would cost. Ian calmly gave him the $1 million figure. There was another pause and then the man said, "Well, a million dollars really isn't that much money, anymore."

We were a million dollars shy of the million dollars we'd need to buy the land, but no more than two weeks later, this same man sent us an email committing to give us the million dollars and he said we should start figuring out how to buy land in Africa.

WHAT? Who does that?! I looked up at the sky for skywriting that day, but realized God's goodness had already been spelled out for me — that million-dollar check was God's handwriting. I immediately repented for my general snottiness toward the idea, apologized to Ian, and asked his forgiveness for not supporting him the way he always supports my crazy ideas. I then gave thanks for the clear and unfettered direction our lives were about to take.

In 2009, we received the check, bought the land, had a dedication ceremony for "Project Canaan: A Place of Hope" and began clearing.

Let me try to explain in layman's terms what this land looked like: It was bush—African bush. There were no roads, no river, no water, no fields, no buildings, no electricity—no nothing. What it did have was dense bush with lots of thorns, rocky soil, old graveyards (that weren't to be moved), snakes (lots of poisonous and terrifying snakes), wild pigs, monkeys, and not-so-friendly neighbors. Roughly 1,500 of the 2,500 acres were a series of mountains and 1,000 acres were closer to flat (but "flat" would be a wildly exaggerated word).

God may have made this plan clear, but it was still crazy.

First things first: We hired some young people from Kenya whom I had met in 2003 and they came down to start clearing the bush. We built the Farm Managers Building first and the chapel next—the first building for a place in which to live and the second to remind us all why we were doing what we were doing. The next task was to clear some land for fields and get our first crop of maize (corn) planted before the rains would come in November. This meant buying a tractor and hiring a bulldozer to push over the bush and tear up the land. Then a team of people had to walk behind the tractor to pick up rocks and put them in the trailer to be hauled away (and later used to beautify all of our buildings with stone cladding from the farm). This was backbreaking, body-tearing work and the Kenyans did it without complaint day after day, week after week, month after month, working alongside a team of Swazis who were working their first job.

Some liked it, some didn't and human resources are always a challenge, but the Kenyans endured and we got a crop in the ground before the rains. While they were clearing and preparing the land, two dams were built to catch the upcoming rains and capture the runoff from the mountainside once the land had been saturated. A borehole was drilled beside the second dam so that we could get the water from the bottom of the dam and irrigate our fields of maize.

Over the next couple of years, we focused all of our efforts upon putting in the infrastructure needed to fulfill the rest of the vision for the land, which included bringing in electricity and putting in roads, backup generators, and a water filtration system. Our goal was to become self-sustainable, which by our definition meant to be able to provide all of our operating costs from the production, sale, and income generation from the property. Donor funding would then only be necessary for capital projects. We had a sophisticated drip-irrigation system installed and 100 miles of drip tape rolled out over 30 acres of fields, allowing vegetable crop production to begin even before the rains fell.

No one enjoyed eating his vegetables picked from our own fields more than Ian! Project Canaan started to turn green, food was being produced, and there was a glimmer of hope in a tiny corner of a tiny kingdom in a tiny corner of the world.

In 2012, we opened the El Roi home for abandoned babies, which you will hear much more about in Chapter Three. A few months after our first baby arrived, the Maxwell family packed up and moved to Swaziland. While the farm could be managed without us and the infrastructure could be orchestrated from the U.S., we felt strongly that we needed to be onsite and hands-on when the babies started to arrive. Getting processes, schedules, and training in place was critical, and while we don't want to raise these children as Canadian or American children, we do want them raised with respect (not being beaten) and given lots of love.

Don't get me wrong. It wasn't like we just said, "Oh, there are babies there, so we need to move quickly." No, it had been planned a year in advance. We knew that Spencer would have graduated from high school and we were told that there was an excellent private school Chloe could attend in Swaziland. We announced to our friends and families that we planned to move to Africa and so started the long and sometimes tenuous journey.

I mean, really, how does one just move to Africa?

Well, you plan well, pack well, give lots of stuff away and *pray!*

On May 31, 2012, the Maxwell family got on a plane and, on June 1, 2012, we became residents of Swaziland, Africa. The next chapter of our journey began.

Remember the story of the burned child at the beginning of this chapter? Let's call her Barbara for now. The same day that she was discharged from the hospital and was taken with her mother to the women's prison, I received a phone call from the prison social worker. She asked me if we had room for a 6-week-old baby at the El Roi baby home. I was having lunch with some dear friends from the Egg Farmers of Canada and asked them, "Who wants to go with me to pick up a baby?" All four men quickly stepped up to the task, though none of us had any idea what we were going to encounter in the hours that lay ahead. We got in the car and made the short drive to the women's prison.

Once we arrived, we left our watches, rings, phones, and other belongings in the car, only entering security with a single piece of identification. The large steel doors were opened to let us in, closed loudly, then locked securely. I think my guests were wondering what they had gotten themselves into.

In the commandant's office, a tiny baby, wrapped in many layers of clothes, was placed into my arms; her face seemed odd to me. It was as if her face was twisted or splotched with paint. As my eyes refocused to see the badly burned face of a 6-week-old baby, I was horrified. All protocols were thrown aside and I quickly undressed her on the commandant's desk to see what was lying beneath the layers of clothing. I looked at the social worker and then to the commandant and asked what had happened to the baby. They shared the tragedy that I described. When they asked, "Janine, can you please take this child to Project Canaan and give her a home and hope for the future?" My unequivocal answer was "yes." This precious little baby became the 78th child to be placed with us through Social Welfare.

Barbara came home with us that night, held in the arms of the three middle-aged men sitting in the backseat. They were trying to give a bottle to a baby who couldn't suck, because her nose had melted and she had to breathe through her mouth. That night we became her family and Project Canaan became her home. That day made an impact on all four of us; it forever changed our lives and helped solidify our commitment to assisting the children of Swaziland.

When our medical team assessed Barbara the next day, we could see that all of her wounds had healed nicely, including the place where her big toe had been amputated. However, she struggled to eat and started getting pneumonia frequently, causing emergency trips to the private hospital in town. Time after time she was discharged, only to be readmitted a week later as the baby formula was ending up in her lungs, causing new bouts of pneumonia. We knew we had to find a better solution.

I reached out to our friends at the Global Medical Relief Fund and they immediately offered to bring Barbara to the U.S. for reconstructive surgery by the team at the Staten Island University Hospital. Over the next two years, Barbara would make two long trips there as surgeons amputated one finger and successfully reconstructed her nose, eyes, lips, cheeks, and smile.

Today Barbara is a feisty, determined (some might even say stubborn) girl whose smile is absolutely perfect. She's happy and doing well in school—a miracle indeed. When I tell the story of Barbara, it often ends there, but not today. Today I would like to talk about Barbara's mother, with whom I have maintained contact (and even a friendship of sorts) since the first day I met her in the prison.

When she handed me the bundle of blankets that contained her burned baby, she was a broken person. Her skin was grey, her eyes were red and empty and her cheeks were permanently stained with the tears of a mother who might never stop crying. She was almost invisible and certainly wanted to be. She handed me the bundle, and after I finished examining the baby, I looked back to where she had been standing; she was crumpled on the floor. I crouched down and asked her what had happened to the baby. It was then that the story unfolded in front of me and my friends from Canada. She slowly and very quietly recited each step of that horrific night and early morning only a few weeks earlier. She sobbed as she disappeared in her mind back to the wee hours of the morning when the horrendous crime had been committed.

She stopped short of telling me how she was sent down into the crime scene to fetch the baby, who was presumed dead, and I didn't have the courage to ask. I only learned that part of the story many months later when a police officer brought another baby to us and asked to see the "burned baby." I asked which one (sadly) and when she described Barbara's story, I asked how she knew it. She explained that she was one of the police officers who tied the rope around the young girl's waist, sent her down into the pit and then took the baby to the hospital.

I asked the young mom why she had done it. Why did she give birth in a pit latrine and then attempt to murder the child? The lengthy answer, summarized by me into one simple word, was "hopelessness." She recounted the age-old story of a man telling her that he loved her and wanted to marry her; all she had to do was have sex with him. So she did and then, when she told him she was pregnant, he denied even knowing her and refused to speak with her. When she finally dared to confess her predicament to her family, she was shunned. She already had a 2-year-old child from another man "who loved her" and that toddler was severely disabled from cerebral palsy. How could she possibly bring another unwanted child into a home already strained and possibly even cursed?

It is common in the Swazi culture for a woman to have a baby with a man to prove she's fertile prior to getting married. In the olden days, having many children would show a man's strength and wealth, so the more wives and/or girlfriends he had who could give him children, the better.

Before you judge this practice, I ask you to imagine children as your 401K savings plan (if you live in the U.S.) or your RRSP (if you live in Canada). Swazi children (in theory) are the ones who will help care for you in your old age, fetch your water, plow your fields, and plant your maize. That's not how things work anymore and now, there are thousands of unplanned pregnancies every year in this tiny kingdom of about 1 million people.

I was told that someone in the young mother's extended family had arranged for bail to be made and the E3,500 ($235) was given to the mother's sister to make the payment, but, alas, she went and spent the money elsewhere. The young mother sat in jail for the next four years (with her disabled eldest daughter, because no one at home would care for the child and the police decided she should be in jail with her mother).

Every now and then I would receive a phone call from an unknown number and it was this very broken and hurting mother. She said I was the only person who would take her call and be kind to her. She asked me to visit a few times and I did. We even brought little Barbara to see her mother before heading to the U.S. for surgery. While my mother's heart bled for the pain, shame, and guilt that Barbara's mother endured, I had to watch my own feelings of protection of Barbara herself, as we are her legal guardians. We are her family and have gone to great lengths to help her heal physically, emotionally, and spiritually. Still, healing has to start with forgiveness, and while Barbara is too young to forgive her mother, I could offer that to the mother for her benefit and peace of mind. She cried, but they were tears of sadness and remorse, not hopelessness and death. We talked about forgiveness and repentance. It was very clear to me, on every occasion we met, that she was deeply sorry for what she had done.

Four years later another E3,500 ($235) was obtained and this time used to pay her bail, so she was free to go home. She is still awaiting trial at the time of this writing, but we assume she will not get more time than she has already served. Her life has completely changed and she has been transformed. She now travels around the country speaking at churches, educating young girls, inspiring anyone with ears to hear about the power of forgiveness by her Lord and Savior, Jesus Christ. While writing this chapter, I received a call telling me that Barbara's 6-year-old sister, who had spent four years in prison with her mom, passed away in her sleep. Jesus uses Project Canaan to bring hope to the hopeless.

CHAPTER TWO

Hunger: Focus or Fail

Staying focused is a challenge for many people, myself included, but when you are in any kind of business, focus is key to success. This is certainly no less true when you are running a non-governmental organization (NGO) or charity. It just seems *really* easy to get off track, side-tracked, or suffer from "mission drift," as authors Peter Greer and Chris Horst describe in their book of the same name, when you are serving in a developing nation. Priorities trump other priorities, plans for getting something accomplished during the day could be wiped out by a seven-hour drive for an emergency baby pickup, an unplanned meeting at the Chief's Royal Kraal to discuss a rise in violent crime or a minister in the government shows up at the gate to discuss the $1 million water plan he'd like us to fund for his community.

Some distractions seem more reasonable than others.

Then, there is the never-ending list of people who ask us for food to feed their children, for school fees so their children can go to school, or for money to buy their children uniforms. All are reasonable requests, but all require time, money, and emotional energy.

Our business background taught us that we can't be all things to all people, so we needed to make a plan that would keep us focused on the areas in which we were being called to serve—specifically feeding hungry children, caring for orphans, helping to alleviate poverty, and provide solid education. This "written in stone" philosophy has kept us on the straight and narrow, helped us navigate the complicated world of living amongst the needy, and also angered many well-meaning donors who envisioned different plans for this ministry. On occasion, as you'll see, we make a few exceptions to our own rules.

I remember when we were first called to this ministry and questioned *why* God would choose us out of the seven billion people on the planet. I could understand Him choosing Ian, because he's always calm, cool, collected, a peacemaker, a hard worker, a lover of spreadsheets with his degree in economics. Ian could add value to a ministry or business of any kind. He has "transferable skills," as we say in the business world. I, on the other hand, am a bit more hardwired, swift to jump in, quick to get excited about a new idea, and ultimately love a good logo and clever tag line—a fairly narrow set of gifts, with little actual talent to create something. We both loved Jesus, but neither of us was the "pastoral type" person.

What was God up to?

Then one day, as we were doing a *Heart for Africa* branding session, I realized that I *do* have something to offer: I know how to build a brand and keep everyone focused on what we do and what we don't do.

Project Canaan is a place of **HOPE**: **H**unger, **O**rphans, **P**overty, and **E**ducation. There are others who work in these areas, but with significant differences. Many people work in the area of hunger, but they don't do what we do. There are many who work with orphans, but they detest and are vehemently opposed to orphanages, alternative care facilities, Residential Care Centers, or children's homes (which is what we have). That is why we've had to define and refine our focus and be able to articulate those areas in a way that, even if they disagree, people understand and respect.

Our hunger initiative has two parts: our farm and feeding programs. Our farm is the lifeblood of Project Canaan and has many facets to it. We have 30 acres of fields that have drip irrigation for watering. We mostly grow food for the children's campus consumption and then a lot of vegetables that we sell to the local market. Eswatini imports 95 percent of its fruits and vegetables, so it is very exciting to us to be able to grow food people want to buy and eat and to be able to provide it without the importation costs. In 2019–2020 alone, we grew more than 264,554 pounds of beetroot (beets). In addition to the irrigated fields, we have 140 acres of dry fields we use for maize silage and hay production for our dairy.

In 2015, we decided to build a greenhouse so that we could grow things that needed more TLC than field crops (i.e., strawberries) and that we could grow through hydroponics by using 60 percent of the water needed for field crops. This is a project that is very near and dear to our hearts.

This .6-acre greenhouse is complete with a climate-controlled, water-cooling system, where we are able to grow our kitchen vegetables for the children's campus, including lettuce, tomatoes, cucumber, peppers, cabbage, and fresh herbs. We sell all these fresh items to our workers at a great price and also to the local golf resort and markets.

While we were building the greenhouse back in 2015, the rains began to slow down, and little did we know that we were heading into the worst drought in sub-Saharan Africa's history. In fact, by the time the greenhouse was built, we did not have enough water to even grow with hydroponics. A tough decision had to be made and we had to stop all farming until the drought passed or we could figure out another way to get water.

One of the very first things we did after we bought the land was to build dams to catch the rainwater and runoff water from the mountain. That is the water we used to irrigate, drink (after being purified), bathe, cook, and build. When the rains didn't come in 2016, the dams started to go down and all three of our dams were almost completely dry. It was heartbreaking and scary. We do not have aquifers under our dams, so there was no water into which we could tap through a borehole. We were hearing the same story all over the country. People were raising funds to drill boreholes, but the water table was too low and either had no water or silty water was found. As we drove around the country, we would pass through or over rivers that had not had water in them for months—and now it has become years.

We contacted experts from all over the world to help us solve our problems and, in 2018, we found a solution. I'll tell you more about that in a later chapter. In the meantime, we stopped watering the grass at the children's campus, reduced our personal bathing to every second day (not fun on the really hot days), and prayed for rain. Ian was determined to grow *something* in the greenhouse and then our U.S. friends at North Point Community Church in Atlanta, Georgia, asked if we had ever heard of aquaponics.

Nope, we had not. They went on to explain that aquaponics is the practice of combining aquaculture (fish farming) and hydroponics (growing vegetables without soil) and it only uses 5 percent of the water used on open-field farming to bring seed to harvest. Crop rotation is not necessary and we could get seven crop turns per year versus the three we could get in an open field of the same size. We would be able to grow our leafy greens for the children's campus and sell, while also raising fish, fresh tilapia, which would be a great addition to our diets. There is nowhere in the country of Eswatini to buy fresh fish! It is all frozen and most often with freezer burn, so this was a really exciting new opportunity for us to consider.

When you are a visionary, trailblazer, or entrepreneur, ideas are often met with doubt, criticism, or old-fashioned pushback, especially by well-intended board members a million miles away. That never stopped Ian. He wasn't afraid of taking a risk, doing *a lot* of research, investing in training, and personally investing financially in an idea that was just too good to not try. Imagine if we could still grow kitchen garden items and fresh fish with virtually no water!

In 2016, we started our aquaponics program with the help of our U.S. friends at Emerge Aquaponics in Colorado Springs, Colorado, and we had our first big fish fry on Mother's Day 2019. It was undoubtedly the best fish I had ever eaten! It didn't happen easily and the learning curve was steep, but Ian moved forward with persistence and grace—even when a worker forgot to turn on the pump after cleaning the tank and we lost 500 fingerling fish (eight months of growth) overnight. Ian was gracious when many of the fish got into the pipes leading to the lettuce and ate all the lettuce roots, and also the time the air stones were not properly maintained and 600 of our biggest fish suffocated to death. While discouraged by the loss, Ian always saw these as teachable moments and good learning for all.

In addition to the fields and greenhouse, we have a large packhouse (like a giant refrigerator) that will allow us to be certified for export. In the meantime, it gives us a place for sorting, cleaning, and packaging fresh vegetables. You can imagine how much vegetable waste there would be on a farm—with corn husks, beetroot tops, and kitchen compost. In 2020, we installed a giant worm pit that serves as a giant composter, turning all our waste into beautiful and nutritious manure for the fields. Never in my life did I *ever* think I would be excited about a worm pit. (Well, honestly, I'd never heard of one!) However, my mom was religious about composting everything she could, so I was in familiar territory—just on a vastly different scale.

Another exciting part of the farm is our dairy operation. We started with six cows and it has grown, through purchase and artificial insemination, to a herd of 130 (that we are hoping to expand again next year). In the beginning, the milk produced was solely used for our babies and toddlers, but then, as the herd grew, we were able to sell the excess milk to Parmalat, a local milk-processing company. Now we produce *all* of the milk our children drink (and they drink a *lot* of milk—by mid-2020 we were sending 300 gallons of milk to the children's campus every week!) and it is pasteurized through an inline pasteurizer at our industrial kitchen. We also make our yogurt daily. In addition to the dairy cows, we have a small herd of beef cattle (mostly made up of the males born to the dairy cows). The beef cattle graze with our rapidly growing herd of hundreds of goats and we have our own abattoir, where we can harvest the red meat used for our children and children's campus staff we feed. This has completely eliminated all purchases of red meat and has saved us a lot of money.

The other *big* project that rounded out the farm was building two barns for 2,500 laying hens each. This project was birthed out of a conversation with a man I met "coincidentally," named Chad Gregory, who happened to be the CEO of the United Egg Producers in the U.S. The UEP offices were "coincidentally" located only a few miles from the *Heart for Africa* office in Georgia and Chad and I became fast friends. Once he heard about what we were doing and wanted to achieve, he knew he wanted to get involved. First, he invited us to Venice, Italy (true story) to speak at an International Egg Commission meeting (I'll bet you didn't know there was such a thing), which is where we met Tim Lambert, CEO of the Egg Farmers of Canada (EFC). Tim and a few EFC members came to visit us in Eswatini and after various meetings and planning sessions, they decided to fully support the creation of a laying-hen operation on Project Canaan. Not only did they commit to raising the funds for the barns and invite partners from around the world to participate, but committed to supporting the operation for five years. Laying hens lay an egg on average every 26 hours, so we get approximately 4,500 eggs every single day, with no turn-off switch, no emergency brake. Needless to say, the children's campus eats a lot of eggs. We also make our own mayonnaise and currently use an average of 250 eggs per day. This laying operation wasn't specifically designed for our consumption; it was to help the ever-growing need for food and good protein and help fill the need for food in the communities around us.

That brings me to our feeding program, the other part of our hunger initiative.

When we first came to Swaziland in 2005, it was announced that Swaziland had the highest HIV/AIDS rate in the world, leapfrogging over Botswana, which had held the record for many years. The country was being decimated by this horrific disease whose best friend was tuberculosis—an evil duo. Hospitals were filled with emaciated people; back then, 90 percent of all people who died in the hospital died from an HIV/AIDS-related illness. An entire generation was being wiped out, leaving sick and aging grandparents and lots of children.

Eswatini is a polygamous society where many men might have six to eight wives. One of the primary purposes of these wives is to provide children (and lots of them) because children are the hope for the future. It's the savings plan for the parents. The theory is that when you are old, your children will plow your fields and fetch water and send money from their jobs in town, assuring that your later years are lived well and under a tree by your homestead.

Back in the 1980s and 1990s, many Swazi men were working in South Africa in the mines, which paid really well, but also required an 11-month continuous-duty contract to be signed. Once a year, the men would come home for a month to rest, see their families, and enjoy their wives. Since many men were enjoying other women while away at work, they would unknowingly bring the deadly HIV to the homestead. Instead of one husband infecting one wife (which was happening all over Africa), he would infect *all* of his wives and then head back to his job in South Africa—often never to return. Families would believe that their husband and father had run off with another woman, but it is more likely that he succumbed to the disease in a foreign land, leaving a plague of horror back at home. As each wife would get sick and die, the children would become orphaned; soon it wasn't uncommon to find dozens of young children and babies living alone in a rural homestead. There were also homesteads that still had an old grandmother (called a gogo) with them, and she was then left to care for the children.

I remember when we lived in Canada, Stephen Lewis, one of my heroes, was the Special Envoy to the UN for HIV/AIDS. He had the brilliant idea of gathering the grandmothers of Canada to go to Swaziland and rally the gogos of the country to stand up and fight for their grandchildren. They helped with training, support, supplies, and as much encouragement as they could muster. That was 15 years ago, so those gogos are either dead or old and frail now. The elderly people of this tiny kingdom used to be the fabric of society, but now that fabric is threadbare and filled with holes. The children are teenagers or young adults—many uneducated, unloved, ignored, and hopeless. Hopelessness turns into fear; fear turns into vulnerability; vulnerability often turns into teen pregnancies, STDs, and HIV/Aids. If they aren't hopeless, they are angry, which also leads to rape, other violent crimes, arson, teen pregnancies, STDs, and HIV/Aids.

When we bought the Project Canaan land, we knew that we wanted to continue helping beyond our own gates and that we wanted to help the children who were in the most remote areas, where there were no Care Points (NGO or government feeding centers). Some children were found living alone in the forest or garbage dumps in town and they were starving to death. That was in 2009 and it hasn't gotten any better due to the situation I described above. What did change was the introduction of antiretroviral medication (ARVs), which could lead to a long, reasonably healthy life when taken properly and with proper nutrition. The hospital floors are no longer lined with emaciated people and they can hold better jobs, but it doesn't undo the damage of the loss of a generation of parents that left behind a wake of orphaned and extremely vulnerable children. We even have a commonly used acronym for them: OVC—Orphaned and Vulnerable Children.

We came up with a plan to partner with churches in the very rural parts of the country to help them feed the children in their communities. We wanted to help the church *be* the church for the children in need by providing healthy and nutritious food. In addition to the church partner being in a rural area, we had three main criteria that the churches had to meet: They had to be a God-loving, Bible-based church, and try to care for OVCs by doing the best they could with what they had. They also had to have renounced the culture of witchcraft and the use of traditional healers. That was the hardest one to explain. They couldn't understand why it was important to us that Christian churches be uninvolved in demonic worship. In the end, we waded through 350 applications and settled upon 30 churches with whom we would partner.

This was an experiment, just like everything else we were doing. We started with delivering ground maize (a staple here) and sugar beans, both grown on our farm. Then we learned about an organization called

Feed My Starving Children (www.fmsc.com) that has a dry, rice-based meal called MannaPack™. We contacted them, applied, and became a partner, receiving our first 40-ft. container with 270,000 meals that same year. Each meal has vitamins, minerals, and nutrients included that our maize didn't have. That was great news!

Then came the egg farmers with their perfect protein in the "humble egg." Now, when a child gets a hot meal from us through their local church, they are also given a fresh, hard-boiled egg to eat right then and there. That way, it can't be stolen on their way home or eaten by a neighbor.

Accountability and transparency are very important to us and we know that both are very important to our donors, so we work very hard to try to keep our church partners accountable and transparent. That is not an easy thing to do when each of them is easily a two-hour drive from Project Canaan. Not only that, but almost all of the pastors of our 30 church partners live and work in town, just going home on the weekends to preach. So we are relying upon volunteers from the church to secure the food we deliver—not sell or eat it themselves—and then cook and distribute it as promised. Those very same people might not be able to read, write or even count, so we have a challenge discerning how many children are being fed.

The church congregations are a testament to everything I have written above with the entire Sunday congregation being 70 percent children, 20 percent women, and 10 percent men. Government estimates are showing that more than 50 percent of the total population are orphans and vulnerable children, and only 52 percent of those children have birth certificates. Those without birth certificates can't attend school because the school says those individuals don't exist.

Try to follow this bouncing ball: Because we have an estimated 70-percent unemployment rate, half a country filled with OVCs, and 95 percent of all food imported (and expensive), there is very little to no food at all at rural homesteads. The food that typically was at home was maize, but because the country has been in drought for three years, no one has planted it. That food upon which they used to subsist does not exist. While maize has very little food value, it, at least, curbed the family's hunger, stopped the crying, and provided comfort.

With no maize, the head of each household is counting upon the school feeding programs to provide students with a meal at school so that they can focus on studies. These programs run Monday through Thursday and then schools close early on Friday so that they don't have to feed the children. That stretches the food longer, but it is even running out early. In 2019, many schools reported that their government food allocation (which is donated by USAID) ended as early as August and as late as mid-September, leaving all children in school without a single meal in a day.

Remember, 48 percent of the country's children aren't even in school because they can't get a birth certificate. (That is a UN Human Rights violation that the government is trying hard to resolve.) Let's summarize this way: 50 percent of the population is children and 50 percent of them don't have birth certificates. That is approximately 250,000—out of a population of one million—children who aren't in school.

Our delivery driver (and assistant) drives 2,200 miles every two weeks to deliver MannaPack™ and hardboiled eggs (that have a special preserving treatment, allowing them to be unrefrigerated for up to 30 days) to each of our 30 churches. Each church receives a delivery from us twice a month and we also deliver MannaPack™ to many of the social welfare offices to, at least, provide a food pack for children who come to them starving. As part of our 10th-anniversary celebrations in 2019, we decided to visit all of our 30 church partners and do "well-child checks" on the 3,500+ children we feed every week. We measured each child, weighed them, took a head circumference of children under the age of 3, and then plotted their status on a growth chart. What we discovered was *malnutrition* and *stunting* even where we were feeding! A recent government statistic revealed that one in four children in the country had severe malnutrition or stunting, and our small survey of 3,500 children more than proved that statistic to be accurate, if not low. We gathered together and prayed about what we were to do next and that is how our 2020 Hunger Initiative came to be.

The 2020 Hunger Initiative kicked off in July 2020; intending to eliminate malnutrition in the 3,500 children we were feeding. To accomplish this, we looked for partner churches and organizations (i.e., Rotary, other service clubs, schools) in the U.S. and Canada who would commit to a two-year partnership with one of our churches in Eswatini. The partnership would include funds to allow us to import more MannaPack™ from FMSC. It would also enable us to increase our laying hen production to feed children seven days per week rather than just on the weekend when most of our churches cooked. With the growing number of OVCs, combined with reduced school feeding programs and no food at home, it seemed logical that we would need to feed seven days a week to be able to achieve our goals.

Our plan is to do an annual well-child check on each child to assess the success of the program and perhaps look for more churches with whom to partner in Eswatini. There will be more children in need of food for the foreseeable future.

People, who are not churchgoers, often ask us, "Why are you partnering with churches?" The answer is simple. The church is everywhere in Eswatini, whether they meet in a building or under a tree. Almost everyone attends church and so it is the easiest and most practical way to reach children in need.

We are continually reminded of the need to remain focused. Our hunger initiatives are designed to produce food and feed children. When we are visiting our church partners, it is very easy to be overwhelmed by the desperate need we see in the country; we want to help everyone we meet, but that is just not possible. Not only is the need too great to provide food security, birth certificates, and education and solve parentless homesteads, child rape, domestic violence, ritual killings, and Swazi GOLD dagga (weed). There is no way that we can assist in all of the problems we see every day.

The government is doing what it can to address each of these issues, but it is an uphill battle. Even if we do choose *one* family to help, because it is in such desperate need, we often fail to truly understand what is at the core of that family's problem and if our good intentions will cause a bigger problem.

Let me give you one example of that happening.

There was a family that our team found in a community not far from

Project Canaan. It included a husband, a wife, and two very small, severely malnourished children. They lived in an old, torn-up tent that provided some protection from the sun, but let the rain pour in at will. The parents cried out for help because they were all suffering badly and the visiting team wanted to help that family. What's wrong with helping the one in front of you, right? Well, we did a little more digging in the community to learn that they were indeed in need. They had no extended family to help them out and the children were suffering. While we were doing our research, we provided them with MannaPack™ and eggs to help the family stabilize.

We then decided to help build them a very simple, one-room building with concrete blocks and cement. It would have a door, a couple of windows, and a roof. We would provide the supplies and the man himself said he could build it and neighbors would help. We proceeded with the plan, feeling that this was a good exception to our rule of staying focused on feeding and not building houses or churches or digging boreholes or any of the other things we are regularly asked to do by well-meaning visitors. I got regular updates and photos as the room was being built.

Then I received a phone call, not more than a month after the home was built, telling me that the man felt like a "big man" now that the "white people" had built him a home. He got drunk and beat his wife to a state of unconsciousness and she was hospitalized. The two children were taken up the mountain to extended family and now we haven't seen them in several years.

Part of me wishes we had stuck to our own rules and only provided the food, but then I look at scripture. It tells us to help the poor; those poor children would have died from the weather sooner than later.

Anyone who serves in a developing nation understands this pull. There is a popular book called *When Helping Hurts* and the subtitle is *How to Alleviate Poverty Without Hurting the Poor . . . and Yourself.* It's a good read for anyone grappling with these same questions and for those of you who have been told no by the people leading ministries "in-country," who won't let you do what you want to do.

I recall the first time I did something like that; I too was well-intentioned and my heart was in the right place (I think). During my first trip to Africa, I was visiting a children's home in Kenya and there were about 500 children there at the time. The home is a two-hour drive from Nairobi and I had the brilliant (in my opinion) idea for us to go to Nairobi, rent a freezer truck (how hard could that be?), buy giant buckets of ice cream, then return and give all the children ice cream. I could see it in my head: two to three scoops piled high on a pointy-shaped cone, with chocolate dripping down over the strawberry onto the vanilla. It was going to be sticky and beautiful and fun because most of these children had never tasted ice cream before. I approached the director of the home with my idea and offered to fund the entire adventure. He paused, smiled at me and confirmed what a good idea it was; then suggested perhaps we could use the money to give the children meat since they rarely had a piece of meat to eat.

In an instant, my whole perspective changed. From that day forward I have tried desperately to see the world around me through other people's eyes, rather than my own—and, of course, to think before I speak. I immediately agreed to buy a "fatted calf" for slaughter and then attended the slaughtering and carving up of the bull. It was like watching surgeons work on a patient with incredible skill, technique, and very little blood! Within a couple of hours, the hide was drying on a tree (to be made into children's drums), the best parts (brain, eyeballs, organs, tongue, and private parts) had been distributed amongst the butchers, and the meat and bones were in giant pots starting to cook overnight. The whole experience was life-changing for me and one I'll never forget.

Little did I know then that just a few years later, I would live on a farm in Africa where we slaughter our own cows, carve them up with electrical equipment, and have some say in who gets all of the "best parts."

Ian's dream of having cows on the land became a reality and soon we'll be making our own ice cream for the children from the dairy milk. Maybe that whole event in Kenya was both a prophetic and teachable experience for me.

CHAPTER THREE

Orphans: The Chosen Ones

Our hunger initiatives got underway and we wanted to have the farm well established before building a home for orphaned or abandoned babies – but that wasn't God's plan, nor was it His timing. There was an urgent need for a baby home to be built, but, living in Georgia, I didn't feel the urgency. It was God's urgency, as soon became apparent.

We had a dear group of friends in Cape Girardeau, Missouri, who came and served with us in Swaziland in July 2009. Shortly after their return home, we received a call that my friend Teresa Birk's son had fallen in their backyard pool and drowned. I have no words to properly describe the grief and heartache that followed, nor could I provide any words to share my friend's pain and suffering. What I can tell you is how that community rallied around that broken family, changing forever the face of Project Canaan. Raelenna Ferguson contacted me and asked how much it was going to cost to build the baby home. I told her I had no idea because we hadn't designed it yet; we had no plans to bring in children until the farm was set up and we had more infrastructure. She explained that she and her community wanted to raise funds for the baby home in honor of Jared Birk's passing, so I needed to give her a dollar amount.

I couldn't. She pushed. I pushed back.

She won and we became fast friends.

We began working on the design for a home for 20 abandoned babies and reached out to our friends at Bullrushes, the baby home connected to Watoto Village in Uganda. With their help and the generous financial support of our new friends in Cape Girardeau, miraculously, the El Roi Baby Home was ready to open at the end of 2011. We hired and started training staff.

Then, we waited for our first child.

On March 1, 2012, Ian happened to be at the top of our mountain with our friend (and landscape design genius), Pete Wilkerson, when I received a call in the U.S. from the baby home ladies in Swaziland, who told me that our first baby, a boy, had just arrived! We were praying that our first arrival would be a boy so that we could name him Joshua—in the Old Testament, the first person to enter the Promised Land of Canaan after 40 years of wandering in the desert. I screamed and called Ian in Swaziland to tell him to get down the hill.

Oh, what a day of celebration that was!

My next call was to Teresa to tell her that the baby home built in honor of her little Jared was open for business. Afterward, I called Raelenna to tell her she was right—and again to repent for my lack of faith. I thanked her for her determination and love.

That is how the El Roi (pronounced El-Row-ee) baby home came to be and how our orphan initiative began. The name El Roi is the Hebrew name for "The God who sees," and it seemed appropriate as we believe it is God who sees the baby who is abandoned, and He also sees the mother who is abandoning the child and loves them equally.

When we opened the baby home, we had a unique plan and platform—and we were focused. For several reasons, we decided only to accept children under the age of 12 months. (That later moved to 24 months, which I will explain.) First, there was a need for a home for abandoned babies. It seemed that every couple of weeks there would be an article in the national newspaper about a baby being dumped in a pit latrine, found in a plastic bag on the side of the road, or left outside a neighbor's house. These children would be taken to a government hospital and some would move to the halfway house, which eventually filled to overflowing (with none of the children ever moving out). Some of them lived (and died) in the hospital. There are, even to this day, severely mentally and physically disabled adults living in the children's ward at one hospital. They are almost 30 years old and have lived there since they were abandoned as babies.

Most orphanages don't take babies under the age of 3 or 4 because they are expensive (diapers, wipes, formula, specialized care). Babies can get very sick and die quickly. It's a much higher risk venture than accepting children who are toilet trained, walking, and talking. The need was great for a home for abandoned babies and, at that time, there were other orphanages that would take older children. All of those homes are now full.

The second reason we took this approach was that we were getting them young, and while they might have sustained trauma in their young lives, they were less likely to have been traumatized, sexually assaulted, or physically abused if they were under the age of 1. That has not always been the case with our babies, but 50 percent of the children we receive are less than 30 days old, so their days of trauma are very minimal. (We did receive a newborn baby who had been in a pit latrine for *five days*, but the mother had wrapped her in a big fuzzy blanket, so she was warm and didn't have a lot of direct exposure to human waste. She did require some medical care, but recovered quickly.) We felt that, by only accepting babies, we would be able to have the maximum impact on their lives, giving them a better future.

Another thing we decided early was that this would not be an orphanage; our children would no longer be orphans once they came to us. We would be called a Children's Home. After much research and advice, it was recommended that Ian and I become "Mom and Dad" to the children so that they have a mother and a father figure in the family and ultimate authority to the home. The hired staff would be Aunties, Uncles, Big Brothers, Big Sisters, and even Grandparents. In siSwati the word for mom is "make" (pronounced *mah-gay*), dad is "babe" (pronounced *bah-bay*), uncle is "malume" (pronounced *ma-loo-may*), auntie is "anti", brother is "bhuti" (pronounced *bootie* ☺), sister is "sisi," grandmother is "gogo" (pronounced as it looks) and grandfather is "mkhulu" (pronounced *mmm-koo-loo*).

All in all, we are one big (and ever-growing) family. This works very well with Swazi culture because, in a polygamist culture, children call all of their father's wives "make" and, while they do have a word for aunt and uncle, they don't typically use it in a homestead. I was bewildered by this in the early years because someone might say their mother had died and they had to go home for the funeral; but then, a month later, their mother would die, again. I remember thinking: "Do you think I'm stupid and forgot that your mother died last month? Sheesh!" In fact, an aunt had already died and then another aunt's death followed. In this culture, there is also the "small mother and small father," who may actually be a brother or sister to the parent; in North America we would call them an aunt or uncle.

My point is that there are enough confusion and extended families in Swazi culture that our big family of aunts, uncles, brothers, and sisters seems quite normal.

We are just one big, happy family.

Let me explain how children come to live at Project Canaan and become our children:

His Majesty the King appoints a Prime Minister (PM) and a Deputy Prime Minister (DPM). The PM is the head of government (under the King) and leads the Cabinet. The DPM is under the PM and is responsible for the Orphans and Vulnerable Children (OVC), elderly, and disabled members of Swazi society. It's not a job for the faint of heart. The DPM has Social Welfare offices in all four regions of the country and in some government hospitals as well. When people have what is referred to as a "social problem," they go to Social Welfare for help. Social Welfare officers are trained to counsel, encourage, and even pray with their clients. Amid the myriad impossible cases and situations that they face every day, these officers can also be asked to mediate family issues, scold a man for impregnating too many women, scold a deadbeat father for not paying child support, and place children in orphanages and children's homes.

In one case, a baby was dumped in a pit latrine and the mother was known to the police. Social Welfare was asked to find the baby a place of safety and that is how she came to us. In a typical case, the police write a report, the Social Welfare officer writes a report, and then, they are supposed to go to the Magistrate Court and get a court order to place the baby with us. This can be a challenge because some magistrate judges don't believe in placing children in a children's home. They think a family member should care for and raise the child. I think we would all agree that it would be wonderful if there was no need for orphanages or children's homes around the world. The truth is there are children who need to be taken away from their own families to a place of safety — children who are abandoned with no family in sight, and children who might have been aborted if a social worker had not stepped in and sought help for a suicidal teen mother and her unborn child.

When a baby is placed with us by Social Welfare, we become the legal guardians of the child until they reach the age of majority; in Eswatini that is 18 years old. We, as a family and organization, are committed to these children for life, just as Ian and I are committed to Spencer and Chloe for life. We want them, like our biological children, to eventually finish as much school as they can, then move out to become meaningful contributors to society. We specifically want to help them go from high school to adulthood, preparing them for a bright future that could change their own nation.

With that in mind, we are working on developing "The Bridge Program," which will take them from 18 to 21 years and launch them into society. We anticipate having many people from around the world partnering with us to become coaches and mentors to our kids as high school draws to a close, helping to prepare them for what is next. (I will go into this further in Chapter 11.)

Another benefit of only accepting children under the age of 24 months is that we can plan well for the future. We know that our oldest children will always be Rose and Gabriel and that they will graduate from high school in 2029. At the time this book is being written, they are in third grade, so we don't need to have a fourth-grade classroom built until the school year starts in January 2021. Our ninth-grade classrooms will be built in 2025 for use in 2026. This allows us not only to plan for the future, but to build a reasonably accurate fundraising plan for the next decade.

One day I received a call about a newborn found in a plastic bag and left under a bush. It was a very hot African February day and a man had been walking along a narrow path through a field when he saw a bag in the bushes move. He thought there was a snake in the bag, so he ran to get help from a local store merchant. As they both approached the bag with bush knives (machetes) in hand with a plan to kill the snake, they heard a noise. It didn't sound like a snake.

In fact, it was a newborn baby girl who had been in the bag for an estimated three days. *Three days!* The black plastic bag was tied at the top, but rescuers believe that a dog or some kind of animal must have torn the bag open, allowing the baby to breathe. This poor little 4-pound baby was covered in burns from the plastic bag sticking to her skin from the hot sun and she had open wounds over much of her body. Her face was swollen and scratched, her eyes too puffy to open. The men called the Sidvokodvo police (less than 10 miles from Project Canaan), who picked up the baby and took her to a government hospital. I got in my car, drove to town, and met them just as the nurses were giving the child a betadine bath. She was so tiny and red. Though she tried to cry from the pain, she was too weak for the sound to come out. For privacy, I will refer to this baby as Jamie. Once Jamie had been washed, we diapered her. She lay in a newborn baby tub in the tiny room that was used for a NICU and, for the next hour, I watched little insects come out of her eyes, nose, ears, and other parts of her body. Each time one tried to escape, I squished it on the bedsheet.

While I was doing this and praying over this newborn baby, I saw another infant in the bed beside Jamie; he was also new, born in the hospital a day or two before. He was a chunky little guy but seemed to be having trouble breathing. I watched his chest rise and fall with each breath—and then the breathing stopped. I looked back to my girl, removed a few more insects from her eyes, and tried to process what I was seeing in the bed beside us. I looked back to the baby boy to watch for his breathing to resume, but all was still. I was very much out of my element back then, so I wasn't sure who to tell or what to do. I left the room and found my friend, Dr. Pawelos, and somewhat hesitantly told him that I thought the baby next to us might not be breathing. Surely, I was mistaken. I followed him back to the NICU room; blood and air bubbles were coming out of the baby boy's mouth. Dr. Pawelos did CPR on the little guy while I stood in the corner and prayed for them both, but the baby didn't make it. He died right in front of my eyes.

For some reason, this tiny little baby girl, who was born in rural Swaziland and left under a bush, covered in burns and bugs, lived while the chunky baby boy born in a hospital died. I don't know why, but I do know we are determined, with God's help, to give the best possible future to every baby put into our care.

Doctors in all the hospitals with which we work are eager to discharge babies as quickly as possible because they know that the nurses simply don't have the extra time to care for the little ones. There are no diapers or bottles in the hospitals and they fear the child getting a hospital infection. I remember once being asked by a doctor to come and get a baby who had been in the hospital for several days. She wanted to get the child to a place of safety: the El Roi baby home. The social workers want to make sure that they've tried every possible family solution before placing a child in an Alternative Care Facility (ACF) and so this caused the baby to be held at the hospital for weeks. When no family could be found, I finally got the call to go pick up the baby. After driving for two hours, I arrived at the hospital only to be met by the doctor at the door. The baby had gotten an infection, had a high fever, and could not be discharged. I understood and appreciated her honesty, so turned back around and drove home. The baby died the next day.

Sadly, we receive *too many* babies who are discharged from hospitals only for us to discover when we get them home that the infants have massive ear infections, pneumonia, or even tuberculosis. Part of our protocol is to put every child on antibiotics as soon as they arrive, unless they have come directly from being birthed at a hospital into my arms and brought straight home.

After Jamie, the 27th baby to arrive at El Roi baby home had been on antibiotics for five days and discharged her to our care. To tell the truth, we weren't quite ready for a baby that small with so much raw skin open to infection; we made a quick decision to move her to our house into quarantine. Honestly, I am not sure that we had thought that decision through. It meant a premature baby who really should have been in a NICU ward getting specialized care was now living in our bedroom. Ian and I took turns every two hours getting up and feeding her. Once we got Jamie home, we looked for a place for her to sleep. She was so small she really could have slept in a laundry basket, but I remembered a small crib that my dad had made for my dolls when I was a little girl. It was something that I had kept for Chloe and perhaps future grandchildren. I had no idea why I'd moved it from Canada to the U.S. to Swaziland until we brought little Jamie into our house.

Ian pulled the tiny doll crib out of storage and that became the infant's bed for the next 16 days.

Our goal, other than to avoid madness borne of sleep deprivation, was to get her wounds completely healed and her weight to 6.6 pounds. She didn't quite reach that weight, but her skin was healed when we drove our little princess down to the El Roi baby home and handed her off to the manager. Little did we realize then how much our time with her would deepen our level of commitment to each and every child who is placed with us. As for Jamie's placement, the social worker and police canvassed the area to try to find the mother who had attempted to murder this baby so they could put her in prison, but she was nowhere to be found. Reports were written and Jamie was officially placed with us.

I actually went with the police to meet the man who had found her. I thanked him for saving her life. By the time I met him, she was several months old and I was able to share super cute photos of the little baby girl he'd saved.

Babies are placed with us for all sorts of reasons; not all are abandoned. We have 30+ children who were found in pit latrines, others discovered in plastic bags hanging in trees, some found on the side of a road, or in a bus stop wearing just a diaper.

In the beginning, we only accepted children under the age of 12 months, but that expanded to 24 months for a few reasons. By the time we made that change, we had more experience with babies and staff, systems that worked, schedules that were being followed, and excellent leadership at the baby home.

Then, I got a call about two 8-month-old twins. Their mother had said she wanted to go to town, so she took the little ones over to an auntie's house and left them outside her door believing she'd be home shortly. Sadly, it's not uncommon here to leave young children, even babies, unattended or unsupervised. It was a Friday night and, as it turned out, the auntie had gone away for the weekend, only to return on Monday to find the two babies starving and dehydrated outside her house. Police were called, the children were taken to Social Welfare and I was called. I grabbed a couple of people and we drove more than two hours to the Social Welfare office where I found two children walking around, *talking and asking for food.*

These were not 8-month-old children. They were 18-month-old children! I looked at the social worker and facetiously asked how many languages the children spoke. I pointed out that we could not accept these children because they were too old. She begged me to take them, as she had nowhere else to place them and the police had already left. I was in a jam. We were the ones who made the rules, so technically we could break them, but what did the Lord want us to do? Our home manager and I went around the corner and prayed, asking the Lord just that question.

When we finished, we both agreed that these children were to come home with us—and they did. They were at once the oldest children in our care. From that point on, we moved our age limit to 24 months, where it has remained. This has been very difficult because we have had to turn away many children in need who were 2 and a half years old or older. It's necessary to have policies and stick to them so that you can continue with the path you should be on and plan for the future.

Allow me to explain.

When a baby comes to us who is under 6 months old, he or she goes directly to Kuthula Place (which means "place of peace" in siSwati). That is the home for 1-day-old to 6-month-old babies. Kuthula Place does not have live-in staff; it has day shift and night shift aunties that care for up to 10 babies.

When babies are around 6 months old, they begin to visit the El Roi baby home. This helps them see that there is more to the world than a small roundhouse and little ones that look like them. Once they are ready, they move down to El Roi and live with more than 40 babies who are 6 months old to 18 months old. The El Roi care team is all women and they all live in the house with the babies, but we do have a night shift that comes to feed and change the babies throughout the night while the live-in staff sleep. The babies all sleep in one large room in double-stacked cribs, which are made at our Kufundza (which means "learning" in siSwati) Carpentry Center.

When a baby is around 18 to 24 months old, they start to visit the Labaketsiwe Toddler home (which means "the chosen ones" in siSwati) for a few weeks. They skip their morning nap and have lunch with the toddlers until they are acclimated and ready to move. There are 10 toddlers in a room, sleeping in custom-made small bunk beds also created at the Kufundza Center. Two to three staff members are in a bedroom right beside each of the four children's rooms.

These three buildings are at the lowest of three levels of housing and we call this the Lower Campus. We typically have 40 toddlers at the Toddler Home, and when they get full, the next transition happens up to the Emseni or Middle Campus, which is where our 3-year-old to oldest children live. At the time of this writing, our oldest children are 9 years old and will turn 10 on December 27, 2020. Each Emseni (which means "grace" in siSwati) building has two stories, with 10 children in a room and two staff members in a bedroom attached to the children's room. That is a total of 40 children and eight staff. There is a living, a sitting, and a TV room between the two bedrooms on the bottom floor, and two bedrooms on the top floor, so that 20 children and four staff share a common area to watch television, play games, sing songs, pray, read books, etc.—just like we would do at home with our children. Our cooks cook, our cleaners clean, and our care team provides the love and care that our children need.

On the Lower Campus, we also have two people who do all the laundry for the 90 babies and toddlers who live there, including 600 articles of clothing, sheets, and towels per day! At the Middle/Upper Campus, the staff do laundry while the children are at school. We don't have cleaning staff for our homes with children over the age of 8, as they have a chores schedule and clean the house and fold laundry with the aunties and uncles—again, just what we would do with our own children at home. They are learning to take care of their things, keep the house clean and clean, and take pride in their environment and what they wear. The staff members still iron the school uniforms until students are old enough to do that, too.

We also have a 24-hour security team dedicated to the children's campuses. (There are other security teams around the rest of the property.) Day-shift and night-shift guards walk inside the electric fencing that is turned on after bedtime (lockdown), and there are also security bars on all doors and windows. You might think that the security bars and electric fencing around the children's campus would be enough of a deterrent to criminals and guards would not be necessary, but our female staff have been so traumatized over their own lives that they want us to provide the very best protection for our most vulnerable children. They are indeed a target in a land of hopelessness.

People often ask about our staff-to-child ratio. Kuthula Place has a 3:1 care-team ratio (three babies to one care team member 24/7). The rest of the homes have a 5:1 care-team ratio, but we are closer to a 3:1 total-staff ratio, which includes cooks, cleaners, drivers, supervisors, and senior supervisors. Each house has a senior supervisor and a supervisor to oversee all staff and ensure proper love, childcare, health care, medicine administration, discipline, and safety are being provided. We have a detailed process for giving all medication from HIV/AIDS antiretroviral medicine to daily allergy meds to treatment for cold and flu; all medication must be given by a qualified and trained staff member. A supervisor or senior supervisor must witness the medication being given to the baby or child. Both staff members initial a tracking document on the wall in each house. All medications are kept in a locked cabinet or refrigerator in each house. I believe this is a critical process for anyone starting or supporting a children's home.

I've told you about our rule about not accepting a child over the age of 24 months, but there was a day that didn't work out so well.

In April 2018, I received a call from a social worker with whom we had not worked a lot and he was from a region where we rarely received children. He asked if I had room for two sisters, ages 1 and 2 years, explaining that their mother had abandoned them with their father eight months before. Since then, the father had been locking the two outside of his mud hut each time he left to go drinking. When he came back at night, drunk, he would allow them to crawl back inside. Neighbors had reported this to a local NGO, which then reported the situation to Social Welfare. When Social Welfare went to investigate the situation, they found the children outside the house and the smaller girl couldn't move. They took the children immediately to a government hospital, where doctors discovered the children were almost dead from starvation. Both were severely malnourished and the older one was suffering from *kwashiorkor*. The smallest one had severe pneumonia and both had very bad coughs, so they suspected the dreaded, deadly, and common tuberculosis.

I told the social worker that we could take the children and he offered to bring them to us. Since their office was a two-hour drive away, we welcomed his kind offer. Several hours later, a truck pulled up and we peeked inside to see the two little girls so greatly in need of help.

Well, surprise, surprise, when we pulled the dirty, sleeping babies out of the back of the truck, we discovered there was a boy and a girl. The social worker had told me there were two girls. He apologized and said that the mentally unstable father of the children had thought he had two girls, aged 1 and 2. The oldest child was actually a 3-year-old boy who didn't speak or walk well and was developmentally around 18 months. The youngest was 20 months old, but just weighed 13.4 pounds and was the size of a 4-month-old. While we do not accept children over the age of 2 years, I didn't feel there was any way to turn the boy away; plus, we want to keep siblings together when possible.

Yes, we broke our own rule, again. I can tell you that just 18 months later, both children are doing extremely well and have recovered to complete health. They are small children, but are healthy and happy.

Physical health and developmental markers are always our first concern when receiving a new baby, but mental and emotional health are also critical as we love these children back to life. While I am not an expert in early childhood development, I am an expert at being an adopted child. I was raised by parents who didn't give birth to me, but raised me to be who I am today. I realize that not all adopted children had the same wonderful experience I did and I am not speaking for all adopted ones, but I can say that my parents were intentional in the language they used with me and in helping me find my identity within the family. Likewise, I am being intentional with the Swazi children God has chosen to place with us through Social Welfare.

My parents always used the word "chosen" with me and I truly felt chosen. I knew I was special, because not only had God chosen to put me in the Willis family with those parents, but Bernice and Russ also got to choose me to be their daughter. Sometimes, as I was growing up and "friends" teased me about being adopted, I quickly responded that my parents got to choose me, whereas their parents were stuck with whatever came out of their mom! I really believed that.

Some of the children who are placed with us through Social Welfare are single or double orphans (having lost one or both parents), some are abandoned babies and some were born to poor or young mothers who simply couldn't care for them. My birth mother was 15 years old and simply couldn't care for me. The difference is that, in 1891, the Children's Aid Society of Ontario, Canada, was founded, providing a resource for my 15-year-old mother to put her baby up for adoption in 1963. She didn't have to dump me in a toilet or leave me in the forest or at a hospital or on a church doorstep. She was directed to this resource and took advantage of the opportunity to provide me with a chance for a future that she could never give me.

I have met my birth mother and thanked her for doing what she did; I assured her that I had a wonderful childhood and that she made the right decision. Sadly for her, she has never told her husband, children, or family about me, so I remain a secret in her heart until this day; but at least, she has peace in the knowledge that I was chosen by a family who loved me well. Eswatini does not currently support local or international adoptions and many young girls don't know that they can go to Social Welfare for help; that is why so many babies are found abandoned.

Here's what I see: Their earthly mother (and father) may have abandoned them, but their heavenly Father certainly never did. He chose a different life for them, one that might not look like a typical Swazi life of living in a typical Swazi homestead with a typical Swazi father, mother(s), and siblings, with no food and little education. Instead, these children have been chosen to be teachers, lawyers, caregivers, doctors, electricians, mechanics, woodworkers, and everything else under the sun that the Lord has planned for their lives. They have been chosen for His purpose, just like each of us. It is our goal to be intentional in making sure that these children find their identity in Christ, rather than their surname or daddy's identity or what school they attended. These children are smart and empowered and there is no reason for them to think that they are "poor orphaned children" being raised at Project Canaan in Eswatini. They are children of the King of Kings!

I am not so foolish to think that we won't have challenges as they grow, but don't all families have challenges? Many people comment that it would be so much better if these children could be adopted abroad instead of living the way they do here; but, would it really be better for them? Not all adopted children are raised in healthy family environments. Not all families are healthy, no matter how rich or educated they are. The fact is that these children are being loved, cared for, educated, and prepared for life to the best of the abilities of a very large family, tribe, and village. On top of that, there is no doubt in my mind that these children will be the future leaders of this Kingdom, and as the wave of HIV/AIDS and poverty wipes out this tiny nation, we believe that these children have been chosen to be the remnant left behind to lead the future.

CHAPTER FOUR

Poverty: Everything is Hard

Anyone working in a developing nation is familiar with the concept of breaking the cycle of poverty; it is a popular idea even in developed nations. The cycle of poverty starts with situations and factors that lead to poverty and, once started, cannot end without outside intervention. When a family cannot earn enough income to provide the basic needs of food, water, clothing, and shelter, then, basic survival is the driver of daily life. Without outside intervention, which includes the introduction of sanitation, education, and healthcare, there is no hope for the cycle of poverty to be broken. The result of this unbroken cycle is hopelessness. Hopelessness leads to moral decay, which leads to the death of the soul and body.

Eswatini is a very poor country, and with much of the working-age group passing away from HIV/AIDS, things aren't getting better. It is estimated that 70 percent of all Swazis are subsistence farmers, which means they mostly live off of what they grow—mostly maize. Maize is a type of corn that is typically white and, unlike my love for a good cob of corn slathered with butter and a healthy portion of salt added, this maize is left on the stock to dry in the sun and then is later harvested and put in a fenced-in bin to dry further. When the kernels are hard, they are pulled off the cob, often by hand, and then ground into a powder and cooked. It is called "pap" here; most African countries have their own word for this staple that was introduced to Africa by the Europeans during colonialism. The closest thing to it in the West would be grits, but pap is stiffer and doesn't have butter, salt, and cheese (all the good stuff) added to it. It is eaten plain, typically using the right hand, and can be rolled into a ball and then used as a "spoon" to scoop up a vegetable that might be on the plate. Pap is cooked over an open fire in a three-legged cast-iron pot. It is common for Swazis to eat only pap for dinner if they are fortunate enough to get a meal at all. Whatever pap is left in the cast-iron pot is eaten for breakfast in the morning. They simply add water and scrape the sides of the pot until a thin porridge is made and breakfast is served.

In 2016, the rains stopped falling and sub-Saharan Africa entered into the worst period of drought in recorded history. In many regions of the country, the rivers completely dried up. Community boreholes no longer provided the much relied-upon water for cooking and there was no way to plant maize. For two years there was not enough rain even to moisten the soil so that seeds could be planted. The country went into a worse situation—when no one thought it was possible to get any worse. People were dying of dehydration because there was simply no water. In fact, it got so bad that the city of Mbabane, where most of the royal family and senior government officials live, had the town water turned off for three to four days at a time, then turned back on for one day so that people could bathe, cook, and clean. This drought marked disaster for an already broken economy and we could sense the desperation in our own community and rural areas where we served. As recently as the end of 2019, many Swazis didn't plant maize because they weren't sure if the rain would continue after it did start to fall; they couldn't risk borrowing money for seed only to have the crop wither and die. Project Canaan planted 45 acres of maize in 2019 and lost the entire crop due to extreme heat and lack of rain.

These desperate times have led to desperate measures, and, sadly, that includes a lot of unwanted and unprotected sex. Young girls have been forced to have sex in return for food or to provide for their siblings. While free condoms are widely distributed throughout the country, most Swazi men do not want to use them; they also like "dry sex," which means any lubrication is removed from the woman so that there is more friction. That leads to tearing, bleeding, and a higher chance of the spread of STDs and HIV. While prostitution is illegal in Eswatini, I still know too many women who have had sex for money so they can pay school fees for their children, and because the men don't want to wear a condom, the women often end up pregnant, again. Interestingly, they don't seem to see it as prostitution. It's simply a business transaction and

I have not sensed a lot of shame about it. It's just a part of life that has been accepted.

Sex trafficking is another way for people to make money. It has become a global phenomenon that has not skipped the country of Eswatini. I remember getting a call from a police officer one day. He told me that they had received a tip about a woman who had a Mozambican girl locked in a house as a sex worker. They were going to raid the house and needed a place of safety for the teenage girl when they got her out. He asked if I could take her. I reminded him that we run a home for abandoned babies, not sex-trafficked teens. He was in a desperate spot as there are no homes or halfway houses in the country that will take a girl like this, so he begged me to help him out. I have a great relationship with this officer and we had saved several lives together; I wanted to help if I could. He promised that she would only be with us for six months because the law is clear that she has to be repatriated within that six-month period. Let me fast forward and tell you that she stayed with us for two years before the same person who trafficked her into the country kidnapped her—yes, *kidnapped her!*—and forced her to go back to Mozambique before she could go to trial. With no witnesses, the case would surely be thrown out of court.

This woman, who I will just call the trafficker, had approached a family friend in Mozambique and offered to take his daughter to school in Swaziland. The man could not afford to put his daughter in a good school and the trafficker said she had a good job and would be happy to help. He had agreed, but instead, the trafficker took the girl on an "adventure." When they got to the Mozambique and Swaziland borders, she didn't pass through the official way, but rather snuck through the bush and paid for an illegal crossing. They hadn't gone more than 100 yards through the bush when the trafficker took the young girl into a shabeen (skanky bar) and fed her alcohol. I was never able to ascertain whether the child was forced to have sex that first night, but that happened very quickly when they got to the main town of Manzini.

This 15-year-old girl was forced to live in a tiny room with a woman she did not know. She didn't speak the local language of siSwati; she only spoke Portuguese (which is not similar). She had no way to communicate with her father, didn't know where she was, and didn't know how to get back to Mozambique.

She was trapped and terrified.

Days turned into months and months into two years before police raided the house. By then the damage had been done. Her spirit and mind were broken, she had full-blown, untreated HIV/AIDS, her skin was crawling with diseases, and she was starving to death.

I distinctly remember the Wednesday afternoon when she arrived at Project Canaan. I asked when she had last eaten and she told us her most recent meal had been Sunday morning, four days before.

Police responsible for handling sex trafficking cases are under the PM's office. I do believe that they tried their very best to help this young lady. They would pick her up and take her to her health appointments, trying to counsel her when she cried and begged to go back to see her dad in Mozambique. Her father still didn't know that she had been trafficked; he thought she was in school in Swaziland until the police were able to drive to Mozambique and find him to share the news of his daughter.

It was only then that they found out the woman trafficker was the girl's biological mother. Since the girl had lived with her father and was never told the identity of her biological mother, she thought the lady had just been a friend of the family.

When I was given this information, a flood of emotions came over me: first anger, disgust, and rage, then deep sadness that has never completely left me. What level of despair, evil, and hopelessness do you have to reach as a woman to not only sexually traffic a young teen girl, but to betray and exploit your own daughter? Was that really the only way that woman thought she could work her way out of poverty?

After police were informed, the mother was put in jail and the young girl was required to stay in the country for the court case. The mother paid bail of approximately $100 and returned to her shop, free until the court date.

The young lady lived at Project Canaan for a year, with me asking the police every month for the court date when things started to get worse. She felt she was a prisoner because she had no money to do anything, the police wouldn't let her go anywhere, and there was no end in sight. She was loved by our staff and she loved us, but she was still stuck, getting more depressed every day and we all felt trapped.

Finally, I got her father's phone number and allowed her to use my phone to call him any time she wanted. They only spoke for a minute or two on any given call, but hearing his voice seemed to help her through the day. I also got permission from the police to pay her for her work (she was an illegal immigrant), which seemed to change everything. She was able to buy treats, her own toiletries (I'd been picking them up for her monthly), and a TV. That not only brought joy to her life but gave her back some pride and dignity that had been stripped away many years before.

Another year passed that way, but the trafficker found ways to threaten the girl into not testifying, and finally, the girl was lured into town and back to Mozambique. While she was happy to be reunited with her father, she was broken, sick, and then got pregnant.

When she was eight months pregnant, the police drove to Mozambique and brought her back to Swaziland for the trial to begin. I sat in the small courtroom for days, listening to this very pregnant young lady tell the details of having been trafficked by her own mother, who sat right across from her in court, glaring. On breaks, they would both leave the courtroom and wait in the same hallway for the trial to resume.

I honestly don't know how she survived the ordeal. I expected her to collapse at the end of each sentence, especially when she told the judge that her mother would sometimes have sex with a man in the same room so that they could get extra money for the thrill of group sex. I almost threw up. The whole trial experience was made even more painful since, with no court stenographers, the aging judge had to write down every word spoken. Because she was speaking in a whisper, he often asked her to repeat herself, doubling the agony for us all.

This young woman was embarrassed and ashamed about what she'd been forced to do and, like in so many of these cases around the world, she was re-traumatized from having to publicly share details. Reporters would then share the specifics of her horrific story to the world in the following day's newspaper.

At the end of her testimony, they decided to rest the case so she could go back to Mozambique and have her baby. Many months later, she came back for the second part of the trial, which was her mother's denial of the charges and counter testimony. That only lasted one day and then there was nothing but silence.

A year went by and I contacted the police officer for an update. He told me the trafficker's lawyer was refusing to continue representing her unless she paid attorney fees. In response, the court awarded an unspecified amount of time to the trafficker (who is out of jail and living her life) to make money to pay the lawyer.

Meanwhile, cases such as these continue to stack up.

Poverty leads to crime. Poverty leads to hopelessness. Poverty kills.

Conversely, employment leads to safety. Employment leads to hope. Employment empowers.

That is why employment is such a critical part of our strategy at Project Canaan and is the focus of our poverty initiative. We employ more than 300 people and our plan is to continue hiring as our programs grow. Government statistics tell us that each person employed in the country is providing for an average of 13 people in the homesteads. If this is correct, then we are helping, through employment, to provide for almost 4,000 people.

A lot of ministries like ours depend on foreign volunteers. We have a different philosophy about this because, as the old adage says, we want to teach a man to fish, rather than just give him fish. People living in poverty have no way to reach even the bottom rung of the ladder to prosperity because it is just too high. However, if they work, they can experience pride, dignity, joy, and hope.

Currently, our largest department on Project Canaan is Khutsala Artisans, which makes beautiful things out of glass beads and wire. The Swazi word "Khutsala" means "hard working," as well as denoting a sense of pride through work. Our goal is to bring hope through beauty, design, and excellence. Not only do we have 100+ people employed at Khutsala, but the product made and sold is a very important part of our goal to become sustainable.

In 2019, the sale of Khutsala Artisans products in the U.S., Canada, and at our gift shop on the farm generated 30 percent of the total operating budget for Project Canaan! One of the strategies upon which we are focusing is having every Project Canaan department either generating income (Khutsala Artisans), providing a service for which we would otherwise pay (Lusito Mechanic Shop, Project Canaan Academy), or producing a product that helps to reduce our operating costs and expenditures (farm, dairy, eggs, Kufundza Carpentry).

As I have said earlier, it's very challenging to make money in farming, but we live in a country where poverty yields hunger, starvation, and malnutrition. We really feel it's important to continue our farming initiative.

Exporting Khutsala Artisans and Kufundza Carpentry products has the potential to help us reach our goal of sustainability sooner rather than later. We often joke that we can't eat beaded Christmas tree ornaments, but their sale can help us put food in our children's stomachs.

I'm a salesperson at heart and a natural promoter. My university degree was in communications, with a focus on journalism. These skills have been very helpful as we share the story of Project Canaan.

In 2013, I was pondering about what else we could make or sell to generate income in order to reduce our dependence on donor support. Somehow, I had the idea of making a Christmas tree ornament we could sell to visitors to give them something from here to take back. People love to go to the craft markets in town to buy souvenirs for friends and family, so why not purchase something that supports us?

I had bought a small angel during one of my many African craft market visits, so I took it down to the farm and gave it to Denis (one of the original Kenyans who came to develop Project Canaan). He's a jack of all trades and I asked if he could find someone who could make something like it. He went to town and found some beads and wire, then pulled a guy from the farm whose father made traditional Swazi shoes. He made a sample, we made some changes that took it up a notch, and then, I took the angel to the U.S. in October 2013 to show it around and see if this idea might work.

I decided to post the photo on Facebook to see if anyone was interested in buying five of them for $50. Within a few hours, we had orders for 600+ ornaments! Ian was in Swaziland at the time, and he, being an operationally driven person, asked me how many I had made. I told him that I had exactly one and it was with me in the U.S. He then reminded me I'd said on Facebook that we would ship them in time for Christmas, so he wondered how I planned to find the necessary materials, people to make them, and ship them to the U.S. within two months. I told him I hadn't thought about that at all, but that our orders had grown to more than 1,000. (That ended up being 1,300 angels ordered by the end of the year!)

Ian went into supply chain mode and tracked down the beads and wire we'd need. Denis found people to train and, when I got back home with the only sample, we launched training and production. It was a grand success and we generated $13,000 in a few short weeks, with a bigger idea on the horizon.

In April 2014, I contacted all of the people who had purchased the angel and shared a photo of the next ornament, which would become part of an annual series. (Everyone loves a good collectible set, right?) It was a hit. We moved from working outside on picnic tables with a dozen people to to working in a large building with more than 100 artisans complete with our own shipping department.

In 2018, we shipped a 20-foot container of beaded animals, decorations, and Christmas ornaments to the warehouse we'd just rented in the U.S. We can now make almost every type of animal into a keychain or 3D home décor: from lions and flamingos to dinosaurs and unicorns. We've created keychains that look like ballerinas and cheerleaders and even specially designed eggs for the Egg Farmers of Canada. In fact, our team has done a great job of providing customized items for many sports teams, school teams, and other groups who want to raise money through the sale of our products.

We have even made a Nativity Set (complete with a wooden manger made at the Kufundza Carpentry shop) and a 13-piece Noah's Ark set. It took four artisans a total of 48 hours, using 192 yards of wire and 56,620 glass beads, to make just one set.

We sold $650,000 in Khutsala Artisans product in one year. That's real money, my friends, with all of the profit going to support our ever-growing number of children. When sales fell the next couple of years, mostly because our customers didn't need more beaded home décor than they already had, we realized we had to start looking for new business opportunities and organizations needing to raise funds.

Feed My Starving Children, who provides us with the MannaPack™ food that we distribute to our church partners, remains our biggest customer, selling our product at their packing sites and in mobile packs all over the U.S. This creates a full circle. We make Khutsala products and ship to them to sell to volunteers who are packing meals; the profit generated from those sales helps buy more food that will be packed by the next group and then shipped overseas to one of 70+ countries around the world that receives their food support, like Project Canaan. And the cycle continues.

Creating and meeting the demand can be challenging. Somewhere along this journey, the bead shop from which we bought our glass beads in Johannesburg closed. By that time, we had started making jewelry at Khutsala Artisans in addition to the bead craft, so our supplier closing was a disaster. They were the largest bead shop in South Africa and we were buying all of our beads and findings (the pieces and parts that go into making a necklace or earring) from them.

We were stuck.

I don't want to oversimplify, but this is exactly what happened next: I was praying about where to find glass beads and a bunch of random findings because I have learned that God really does care about the details. I asked Him for a solution. Almost instantly I sensed that I was to email my friend, Patrick Sun, who was a very successful businessman in Taiwan with factories in China, and ask him if he happened to know anyone who could help. I sat on one of the picnic tables where our artisans work and typed out a quick email to my friend.

Within 10 minutes I had a response! He was thrilled to let me know that he had an office in Yiwu, China, which is literally the bead and findings capital of the world. He told me to take photos of what we needed and send them to him; he would immediately put his team to work. Within 24 hours we not only had a solution provider for everything we needed to buy at a scale that we never would have expected, but this man offered to source and sell everything to us at factory pricing as his way of supporting our ministry. While it would take time to ship from China, we could plan for the future and increase the profitability of our sales exponentially! Within that same year, we received our first shipment of six tons of glass beads in all colors and sizes and Khutsala Artisans was off to the races!

Most of our necklaces, bracelets, and earrings used a local supply of ceramic beads. We were thrilled to be able to support a company that hired rural women to handroll the beads and then bring them to town for firing in that company's kilns. The beads were beautiful, the people were lovely, and the female empowerment and employment were a great bonus. Sadly, their dependability and accountability were not as good as their beads or their personalities, so it became impossible for us to process orders on time. Being undependable to our customers was not acceptable, so we knew something had to change. We had no idea how to make our own ceramic beads, but suspected that was the solution.

One day in the middle of a drought, a group of us, including long-time volunteers and friends, Jere and Janet Scott, were standing on the very dry and cracked basin of Dam #1, praying for rain. At the end of the prayer, Jere was looking down at his feet. Then I saw him cock his head slightly, bend down and pick up a chunk of dried clay. He looked at us and said, "You know, this clay can be used to make ceramic beads, and Janet and I know how to do that."

Well, of course you do, Jere. I don't think that there is anything that Jere and Janet Scott, *Mr. and Mrs. Renaissance,* can't do! They came to our rescue and not only ordered a kiln to be custom made in South Africa, but they also began teaching some of our artisans how to turn Swazi mud into round balls. After being baked in a kiln at 1,940°F for nine hours, these could then be hand-painted with colored glaze and again fired in the kiln for another round. What it yielded are beautiful, handmade ceramic beads that we now call SwaziMUD beads. Every good product needs a brand name and I can't think of a better one than this!

When I find myself overwhelmed by stories I have heard, or if I've had a bad day and the enormity of the project comes into view, I do one of two things: I either go to the toddler home and just love on our forty 2-year-olds, refilling my cup to overflowing, or I go to Khutsala and work on new product designs, using the creative side of my brain. Khutsala also has an air-conditioned office, so when it's 100°F+ outside, it's a great place to work (and the only place to stay cool, other than my truck).

While I am sitting in the office, it is not uncommon for me to hear a light tap on the door, and someone will come and ask if they can speak with me privately. I always say yes, but am hesitant, not because I don't care, but because I know the story will be hard to hear and I likely won't be able to do anything to help. Truth be told, much of the time they aren't coming to me for a solution, but just for an ear to hear and a shoulder upon which to cry. I've had young women come in with bruised faces and eyes swollen shut, hidden by large sunglasses to disguise the beatings they'd endured at home. I've had young men come and tell me they'd just been kicked out of the homes in which they'd grown up, raised by grandmothers after parents died. Once the grandmothers, too, passed away, uncles would decide they wanted to live in the houses. The young men just had to leave.

I've sat and listened to a pregnant woman tell me that she was kicked out of her deceased husband's homestead, where she'd lived with their 6-year-old daughter, because she was pregnant with another man's baby. Even though her husband was dead, she would not be permitted to bring another man's baby into that home. Usually, that is a tactic used by families to reduce the number of mouths it has to feed, but in this case, she was the sole breadwinner. They just didn't care.

One day, a young woman came in and told me she was pregnant and the father was a married man, but she loved him and wanted to have his baby. There was little I could do to counsel her at that point, but I appreciated her letting me know because she lived on Project Canaan. A few days later, I was told that she was in a lot of pain and was taken to the government hospital. It turned out that she was having a miscarriage and lost the baby. Rather than admitting her, the hospital staff had her put her street clothes back on and sent her home. She arrived back on Project Canaan after dark; I called her to say how sorry I was that she had lost her baby.

About an hour later she sent me a text, asking what she should do with him.

"With whom?" I asked. Her answer shocked me.

When she had left the hospital, staff had insisted that she take with her the body of the baby she had miscarried. They had put the tiny, bloody figure in a plastic bag, placed that in an empty rubber-glove box, and then handed the box to her. She had carried that box on the small public bus and then walked four miles to Project Canaan.

I immediately got on my ATV and drove down to see her. When I arrived, she was sitting on her bed with a t-shirt covering the glove box. It couldn't possibly be true, but it was.

It turns out that being buried at your own homestead is very important to Swazis because they believe that otherwise, you won't be able to find your ancestors when you get "to the other side." This young lady was an orphan, so did not have a homestead where she could bury her unborn child. I asked her if she wanted us to bury him in the cemetery on Project Canaan and she said yes. As I got up to give her a hug and leave her room, she asked if I would take the box with me. Ummmm, no! I didn't want to do that, but she was distraught and said she couldn't sleep with him there, so I did.

Later that week we had a modest funeral for this little guy who had not lived to see the world. He never had to suffer at the ugly hand of poverty as his mother had done for most of her life. We buried his tiny body at the Solomon Emathuna (Solomon's Cemetery), named after the first child whom we lost to HIV/AIDS. Not long afterward, she left us to search for someone else, hoping they could take away her pain and suffering and love her. I'm not sure she will find that comfort in the men she'll meet. The cycle of poverty will likely remain and the decay of hopelessness continue to shadow her path.

CHAPTER FIVE

Education: The Most Important Weapon to Change the World

The old khokho (great grandmother) was very thankful that I agreed to take her great-grandchild, the one born to her 15-year-old granddaughter after a family member had raped her. There was no food in the homestead and the khokho was caring for too many children to count. She couldn't read or write, so wasn't able to sign her name on the social worker's report, but she put her thumb on the ink pad and then the line that the social worker was indicating. That would have represented her signature, her commitment, and her way of giving away the toddler, but the ink pad was dry.

That was not the first time I had experienced this situation. In fact, I had learned a trick early to solve the dilemma each time the social worker's ink pad went dry. In a case like that, I would take my own ink pen and color the old woman's thumb until it became blue; she would then make her mark on the paper. *Problem-solving 101.*

She looked at me with tears in her eyes and said, "Siyabonga" ("thank you" in siSwati). I asked the social worker if the tears were the sorrow of having to give this life away. She quickly replied no, that the khokho was so very happy that the child was going to be saved and she wouldn't have to bury another child. They were tears of joy.

Problem-solving is something that I learned not just in school, but also through my unusual life experiences. Truth be told, I can't imagine a life without education. Growing up in Canada, I began my formal schooling with kindergarten at the age of 4 and advanced through Grade 13. (That grade no longer exists.) There was never any discussion in my family about going to university or not; I was expected to go to university and I did.

I took my education for granted and only contributed the amount of work necessary to keep my parents off my back about grades—not a bit more. I loved to read books and write stories and I excelled in public speaking. Math and science were not my strong suits, but I made it through both Grade 13 *Functions and Relations* and Grade 13 *Calculus*. I can explain photosynthesis if needed.

It was just what I did: I went to school. It was my job.

For many years, education was not free in Swaziland (nor in many countries in Africa), so if parents couldn't pay the school fees for a child, he or she simply didn't go to school. And if funds were limited, the "boy child" was always chosen because everyone "knew" that boys were smarter than girls. (You can imagine how I feel about that. *Grrr.*) With the AIDS pandemic wiping out the generation of people who were in the workforce and could pay for school fees, the government started to fund first grade in 2009. That "free education" would be extended each year until seventh grade. To enroll in high school (beginning in eighth grade), students would need to pay tuition.

There are a few things that complicate the education of Swazi children. First, even with free tuition in elementary school, students must still purchase and wear a school uniform including black school shoes. This cost is prohibitive for many students who have lost their parents and are living with a grandparent raising many children.

The second problem, and perhaps an even bigger one, is one we've already discussed a bit: To register for school, you must have a birth certificate. Unfortunately, it has become almost impossible to get one if both parents are not alive and present at the registrar's office. There is little hope for those who have been abandoned (150+ of our children still do not have birth certificates), a victim of rape or incest, or if the father denies paternity.

In North America, it is the hospital that completes the birth certificate; the child receives it before leaving the hospital. That is not the case in Eswatini. If a birth certificate application is not submitted, in person, with both mother and father present, it is denied. According to the United Nations, this is a basic human rights violation and, if the country goes to war or is overtaken, children without a birth certificate are deemed to be stateless; they don't exist and have no rights anywhere.

That is not okay. The UN and African Union have confronted Eswatini about this for years and yet the problem still exists. The DPM's office has been trying to work with the Home Affairs office on the issue, but there is a conflict in Cabinet between the Convention on the Rights of the Child (CRC) and The Births Marriages and Deaths (BMD) Act of 1983.

In a recent document that I received from the DPM's office, the problem was explained this way:

"The right of a child to be registered immediately after birth and be given a name, acquire a nationality and avoid statelessness, be cared for by his natural parents or guardians, as provided by the constitution and entrenched in Emaswati cultural heritage, is seriously compromised. According to the Convention on the Rights of the Child (CRC) children need to be registered immediately after birth. Domestically the Children's Protection and Welfare Act (CPWA) of 2012, requires children to be registered within three months after birth. While the CPWA of 2012 does provide for the registration of orphaned and vulnerable children and gives a specific role to the Central Statistics Office (CSO) to actually collect, analyze and keep a National Register of Orphaned and Vulnerable Children (OVC), there are no clear legal processes or guidelines that guide the registration of Orphaned and Vulnerable Children. The Births Marriages and Deaths (BMD) Act of 1983, does not have provisions for registering OVC."

While Cabinet Ministers (appointed by His Majesty the King) argue about semantics in legislation that makes no earthly sense and with no hint of common sense, almost half of the child population of Swaziland cannot attend school. Then, some simply can't afford high school fees, uniforms, shoes, etc.

While I find myself having deep sympathy, even pity, on the elderly people I meet who can't read or write, I am mortified at the percentage of *this* generation of the population who may never be able to read or write.

Nelson Mandela said, "Education is the most powerful weapon which you can use to change the world." We agree. Without a vision, the people die; but if the people can't read or understand the vision, they also die. That is one of the many reasons that education is so important to us and that the "E" in *HOPE* is critical to the future of the Kingdom and the world. Not only do we have our own formal school on-site for our children, but we also support an adult education program called "Sebenta," which teaches Swazi adults the basics of reading, writing, math, and some critical thinking. We also have a bi-weekly lunch-and-learn-style lesson for all 300+ Project Canaan staff. It's called "Lehora leKufundza," which in siSwati means "knowledge is power."

In 2014, we opened the Project Canaan Academy (PCA) with our oldest children going into preschool at the age of 3. Our head teacher and visionary for the school, Amber VanWinkle, is a long-term volunteer from the U.S. She and her husband Kenny moved to Eswatini a year after we did and she has given our children an excellent education; it is her life's work.

The Project Canaan Academy is a Christ-centered learning environment from preschool through Grade 12. It is specially designed to empower and inspire students to develop to their potential intellectually, socially, emotionally, physically, and spiritually so that they can be the future leaders of Eswatini. The school implements a hands-on project-based approach to instruction and adheres to a philosophy that addresses the needs of the whole child as well as practicing current, research-based education with an emphasis on <u>Howard Gardner</u>'s Multiple Intelligences (MI) theory. MI theory is a way of explaining how children learn. It also emphasizes the diverse abilities of children and the need to assess learning using multi-dimensional evaluations. A child is intellectual, social, emotional, and spiritual. Our plan is to monitor carefully and support growth in each of these facets. We have a commitment to train the solution seekers and leaders who will bring a positive impact to Eswatini, Africa, and the world. The Project Canaan Academy also serves as an educator-training facility that attracts visitors from Eswatini and around the world. Every teacher, mentor, and staff member at our school is involved in groundbreaking and innovative strategies unlike any other educational institution in Eswatini.

Doesn't that sound like a school that can change the future of a nation?

As you have read, we only accept children under the age of 2 at the El Roi baby home, so we don't have older children coming into the program. That has allowed us to be very thoughtful in planning out our school. With our oldest children now starting in preschool, we "only" need to raise the funds to build one classroom each year. (At least that was the plan.) In 2018, during a planning session with our PCA Academic Council, we realized that our kindergarten class of 2019 would have 40 students in it. While that would be considered a small class in a typical Swazi school, it was too many students to provide the best possible education, especially since many of our children are delayed and need a lot of extra help. Therefore, the council decided that we would need to have two classes for each grade, starting in 2020 with our first-grade class. Then, we would need to build two classes per grade each year after that. The older students had a smaller number of students per class based upon how many children were placed with us through Social Welfare in our early years. With this knowledge, we were able to work on a long-term fundraising strategy, inviting people to invest in the future of our children's education, knowing that we didn't have to build it all at once. In fact, we don't need a ninth-grade classroom until 2024 and our first high school graduating class will be in 2029.

Having a long-term plan is helpful when building for a future generation. Many people in the west are thinking about where their newborn baby is going to go to preschool just after the baby is born and then discussing college choices for their first-grader so that they can find agreement on whose alma mater the child will likely attend. Most educated people plan for the future, but if you are not educated, living in poverty, and wondering what you will feed your family the next day, there is no room for future planning. It is a waste of energy.

PCA is not only an education facility for the children who live at Project Canaan, but also serves as an outstanding private school for children who live at the local golf resort and are able to pay for private Christian education. Their fees help cover operating costs, thereby reducing the fundraising required.

We want our school to become self-sustainable, too. I believe in my heart that we have the best school on the continent of Africa (come and see for yourself if you don't believe me!), and our children are excelling in their studies to the best of their abilities. Our special education teachers are very busy with many children with special needs, but we are always amazed at how many of our children quickly catch up to their classmates and are discharged from the special education class. This is largely due to the commitment that the teachers have, but also the commitment of our staff at home, who work with our children to achieve their highest potential. I think it is safe to say that every Swazi, educated or not educated, knows the importance of education, and since almost all of our staff are Swazi, they want to help our children receive what they themselves never got. It is a beautiful phenomenon and I am so very proud of each and every one of them.

Some of our children still struggle in school, mind you. That's not surprising, based on their history and the reasons they were placed with us. I mentioned a toddler at the beginning of this chapter; she is one of the children who may struggle in school for a long time. When I first saw this child, whom I will call Sebe (pronounced *Say-bay*) for purposes of this story, she had been in and out of the hospital for much of her 23 months of life. She was first admitted for a broken arm when she was only a few months old. It appeared to be a spiral fracture, which is a bone fracture that occurs when a long bone is broken by a twisting force. Sebe lived in a very rural part of Eswatini and was taken to a government hospital. While it usually takes a combination of surgery, rest, and physical therapy to recover from spiral fractures, she was plastered (given a cast), prescribed ibuprofen for pain, and sent home. It seemed that just as one fracture would heal, another one would appear and she would end up back in the hospital for more plastering. This cycle continued for almost two years, rendering her right arm scarred, crooked, and without full mobility. The social worker questioned the young mother every time the child was admitted and each time the teen said the child had fallen and broken her arm. The social workers have little access to transport or other tools to help them assess cases of child abuse properly. There is also a sense that "what happens at home stays at home." There is a word in siSwati, "tibi tendlu," which means "sweep under the rug and keep it in the family." This would be one of those cases.

It was in September 2015 that I was first notified of this child. I was told that she had been admitted to the hospital with a broken femur and tibia and that the hospital refused to do surgery on the child until they were assured she would be put in a place of safety following the surgery. They knew there was serial child abuse going on and used the only pressure point they had to stop the abuse. I got in my car and drove to the hospital to assess the situation and discuss it with the social worker. At that point in my history, I didn't have a lot of experience in extreme health or emergency situations. (Sadly, I have *too* much experience in those areas now.) I had no intention of taking the child that day; I just went to discuss what could be done to help.

When I got to the hospital, I found a despondent child who was almost 2 (our upper admission limit) and a young mother who looked detached, mentally disabled, and simply not present. Sebe's leg had been wrapped in a tensor bandage, and while she had to be in extreme pain, she showed no signs of it. She was accustomed to pain and had learned that crying only brought more pain, so she suffered in silence.

I was shocked by what I saw; the doctor, nurses, and social worker begged me to help. They had the X-rays in hand and wanted me to take the child, immediately. "Take her where?" I asked. She had a leg that was severely broken in TWO PLACES, above and below her knee. How could that even happen? While the family insisted that her foot had gotten caught between rocks and twisted, the orthopedic surgeon later told me that it would be impossible to break her leg in that way. What to do?

I agreed to have Social Welfare place the child with us, but she needed immediate help. I had someone call the orthopedic surgeon in town (a three-hour drive away) and ask if we could see him that day. He said yes. I didn't want to take the child for surgery without a court order placing her in my care, in case something unforeseen happened during surgery. I needed to find a magistrate court judge who was available, capable, and compassionate; I made a phone call and found a judge who could help. I took the social worker report (with the khokho's thumb-print signature) and drove another 45 minutes to the magistrate court.

After explaining the whole situation, complete with X-rays of past and current broken bones, the magistrate wrote out a court order, by hand, that placed the child at the El Roi baby home. Then, he informed me that his secretary had retired, so he had no one to type out the order. I saw an old Windows computer (I am an *Apple gal*) in the corner of his office and asked if I could type it for him. He agreed. I stood and typed while this magistrate judge dictated his court order. When I went to print the document, he told me that the printer was broken... *seriously*! I grabbed a flash drive from my purse, copied the document, and asked where I could go to print it. He told me of a quick-print place in town and that is where I went with the social worker who had come along. We got two copies, then went back to the judge and got him to sign and stamp both copies. *Whew!*

It was getting late in the day (I had started my journey early that morning) and I needed to get to the orthopedic surgeon before he left. I thanked everyone involved, drove back to the hospital, and loaded Sebe and her mother into the backseat of my car. I wouldn't have taken the mother under normal circumstances, but hadn't gone to the assessment with anyone else, so needed someone to sit with Sebe in the back seat. I called

Project Canaan to ask for a children's campus staff member to prepare for a long hospital stay and my friend and long-term volunteer, Chris Cheek, to meet me on the side of the road. Only 90 minutes later the two ladies and a load of supplies entered my little car and off we went.

An hour later we were at the hospital and the surgeon was looking at the X-rays. He showed us where her arm had been twisted and broken multiple times in multiple places. Even this Swazi surgeon, who thought he had seen it all, was surprised and brokenhearted at the abuse that this toddler, not yet 2, had experienced.

I was later told that the abuse had mostly been at the hands of Sebe's own grandfather, but getting the truth about such things is always a challenge and fraught with uncertainty. What causes or enables a person to ever hurt a child, much less over and over, again? There are many answers to that question, but I believe part of it is a lack of education.

Sebe's surgery was successful and she came "home" to Project Canaan after a couple of days. She lived in Chloe's room at our house for a few weeks while we monitored the swelling of her leg. She didn't have a hard cast on her leg, yet, and we didn't want to send her to the toddler home with 40 other 2-year-old toddlers who would be very excited and curious about the new girl. A couple of times a day, a small group of girls would come up to visit her, bring treats, play games, and sing songs. Once a hard cast was put on her leg, we moved Sebe down to the toddler home. It took a long time for her to smile and even longer for her fear to go away.

Eventually, we began to see a beautiful, bouncy little girl whose heart was starting to heal and whose mind was beginning to forget all that had been done to her. The long and gnarly scar on her leg and disfigured arm would serve as a lifelong reminder of her past, but the healing deep in her soul is what we are prayerfully pursuing.

Now that Sebe is in school, we are starting to see some of the side effects of her past play out in her learning challenges. She is distracted, pretends to sleep when she is overwhelmed, and just wants hugs all day long. Sebe is getting extra TLC from our special education teachers and staff at home. What I know for sure is that the Lord has a big plan for this little girl's life and she is being perfectly prepared for that plan. I can't wait to see what is in store.

While our children are getting an excellent education, we believe we can also help our adult staff with furthering their education. We have joined forces with a government-sponsored program called *Sebenta* (means "we work" in siSwati), which is an adult education program. It is a three-year, six-hour-per-week course taught by volunteers from Project Canaan. It's a huge commitment for the teaching volunteer and for the students. During these classes, they are learning the alphabet and basic reading. They are also learning their numbers, simple addition, and subtraction. They are also learning some critical thinking techniques, which may seem simple to us, but challenges the learner.

Here are a couple of questions that were on the 2019 Year End exam:

1. I have 85 goats. My brother has 157 goats. How many goats do we have in all?

2. Siphiwo has E200.00 to buy books. The book prices are as follows:

   Basic English Unit 1   − E*18.00
   Basic English Unit 2   − E 20.00
   Numeracy 1   − E 25.00
   Calculate how much her change is going to be.

3. Name two signs of malaria.

4. What do you think is meant by the phrase "pass away?"

E is the short form for Emalangeni, which is the currency in Eswatini.

Another important area under our education initiative is a focus on vocational training—not only training and employment for local Swazis today, but developing programs that will benefit our children in the future. Many of our children won't go on to post-secondary education, but with excellent training in the trades, they can become the best mechanics, master carpenters, or millwrights in the country. Every country needs these skilled trades, especially developing nations.

The very first trade that we focused upon was carpentry; our friend Jere Scott helped us build the Kufundza Carpentry Center (means "learning" in siSwati). Our goal is for each of the men (and women!) in the carpentry shop to get their full certifications to become Master Carpenters. Fortunately, we have an ever-growing list of things that need to be built out of wood, including baby cribs, bunk beds, wardrobes, cubbies, desks, picnic tables, and all sorts of cabinetry in every building we build. They have also learned to spin bowls on the lathe, make African wall art out of scrap wood, and make stunning cheese boards that are sold through Khutsala Artisans. All of these people are fully employed and paid, further supporting our "Poverty" pillar.

We have our own construction team, which has built 70+ buildings in the past 10 years. That team includes electricians, plumbers, welders, and masons, with apprentices learning alongside and behind them. Our mechanic training program includes everything from changing a tire properly on small cars (so they don't fly off the wheel rim as I have had pre-training) to fixing a JCB backhoe, putting new tracks on a Bobcat, maintaining and repairing a D5 bulldozer, and even servicing 200 kVA generators. The mechanic shop is a busy place and a critical part of having a well-running farm and project.

In addition to everything written above, we are very committed to educating our staff on the health and social issues that nearly every Swazi encounters on a daily basis. With that in mind, we have a program called *Lehora lekufundza.* Every second Friday we invite an "expert" to come and speak to all 300+ Project Canaan employees. The speaker circulates around the property, spending an hour with different departments. The health topics include HIV/AIDS, tuberculosis, STDs, birth control, family planning, and hygiene. The social topics include child protection, domestic violence, violent crime, children's rights, and the myths around albinism.

These sessions are mandatory and we encourage a free flow of questions and direct answers. The sessions have caused conflict for some and enlightenment for others. They have shone a light in the darkness and brought some clarity to cultural confusion.

An example of this would be the topic of "The Myths Around Albinism." In many African countries, there is a disproportionately large percentage of the population who have albinism. Different countries believe different things about this, but in Eswatini there are a few beliefs that run deep and wide and were believed by most of our staff until we started these education sessions. Most Swazis believe that a person with albinism (albino) is an animal, not a human. They believe that albinos never die, just disappear. The worst belief (in my opinion) that I have heard is that an albino baby is a very powerful creature — an animal that can be used by traditional healers (witch doctors) to make powerful "muti," a potion made by a healer for the customer to drink to gain power or knowledge. Albino babies are thought to have a lot of power and are often hunted and stolen from homesteads to be taken to the traditional healers and sacrificed to be used to make muti.

Eswatini is not the only African country to believe this. In Tanzania, they don't sacrifice babies. Instead, they cut off limbs (hands, feet, arms, legs, and private parts) of children to be mixed with the muti, and the child lives if immediate medical attention is administered. In neighboring Mozambique, only the head of an albino child is used and the rest of the body gets discarded. But in Eswatini, it is the babies that at the greatest risk—the whole child.

A couple of years ago, I received a panic call from a social worker on the Saturday before Easter. She told me that two cars with South African license plates had pulled into a very remote homestead; some men had gotten out of the car and walked to the door. A young teen girl greeted them and they demanded that she give them the "animal." She didn't know what they were talking about and when she questioned them, they told her they were there to take the albino. Her very own baby, with albinism, lay sleeping inside the house, but she calmly told them they had the wrong homestead and must continue down the road a few kilometers. The men got back in their cars and drove away, while the young girl grabbed her baby and ran to the police station for safety. It was evident to the police and social worker that someone in the community had reported the child to a buyer and they had come to collect the child. During election years, it is said that an albino child can be sold for up to $50,000 in Eswatini!

I find it hard to type this paragraph for you and know it's even tougher for you to read it, but it is important for you to try to understand what we are facing in our day-to-day discipleship of our Swazi brothers and sisters. While learning to read and write is important, so is understanding that some cultural beliefs are misguided and evil.

To help with this educational topic, we invited the Director of the Albinism Society of Eswatini to come and speak to our staff. Her name is Stukie and she was fantastic! She has albinism and was able to answer many questions with great confidence, as well as to assuage doubt and even confirm that albinos do die and that she had personally attended many albino funerals. Her answers were met with skepticism because they went against everything that they had been taught their whole lives, but it was a start. We will invite her back, again, next year for Round Two.

Nelson Mandela wrote, *"The power of education extends beyond the development of skills we need for economic success. It can contribute to nation-building and reconciliation. Our previous system emphasized the physical and other differences of South Africans with devastating effects. We are steadily but surely introducing education that enables our children to exploit their similarities and common goals, while appreciating the strength in their diversity."*

CHAPTER SIX

The Importance of Identity

People are often curious about whether we will tell the children their stories. As you've surely noticed already, there are times I don't identify children so that their privacy is maintained; they won't read their story in my book. Other children in this book have been given different names to protect their identity, but I do believe that, one day, when it's age-appropriate and if they ask, we will tell them the story of how the Lord sent an angel to protect them and even bring them back to life. While these stories are hard to hear, they also serve to provide magnificent testimonies for God's plan for the future of these children.

We recently received a baby whose mother had strangled her own 4-year-old child and then put the child in a pit latrine, where her bones were found months later after an investigation was done by the police. Why did that child die and the baby live? Why was the baby rescued by police and yet the 4-year-old wasn't? We can't know for sure.

Most of us are familiar with the Bible story of Joseph: He had a bad life, starting with being dumped in a dry well by his brothers and then sold into slavery by those same siblings, only to be later imprisoned by his own master for a crime he didn't commit. He spent many years in a dark prison, but in the end, he was rescued, redeemed, and put in charge of all of Pharaoh's wealth and affairs. Joseph went on to save the lives of his own father and brothers who'd tried to kill him. He saved a nation of people, who continue to tell his story thousands of years later.

I wonder if he had a guardian angel with him throughout his life who encouraged him, prayed over him, and helped him choose joy rather than anger at each turn in his life. The dry well, slavery, and prison are all important parts of his story, which ends in healing and forgiveness. If Joseph had handled those situations with anger, hatred, and revenge, his life would have turned out very differently and his story wouldn't be told to this day.

The children who have been saved and brought home to Project Canaan must understand at their very core that the Lord has chosen them to be a beacon of hope and light in a world of darkness. He has chosen them and placed them in this place of safety to grow, groom, and prepare them for lives that will change the nation and the world. In order to do this, I believe that they must not be labeled by their past, but first, find their identity in Christ. Only then will they truly be able to embrace the calling that has been placed on their lives.

There are a few things about which we are intentional as we help build each child's individual identity, starting upon arrival. First, it is the

Swazi name. When we receive a child, there is always a hospital health card, which almost always has a name on it, whether chosen by a parent, grandparent, police officer, or nurse. It is not a birth certificate. We always keep that name for the child and typically add an English name as well. That started in the early days because I couldn't pronounce most Swazi names. We were also getting multiple children with the same first name, so it worked in our favor to have started early giving an English name. Typically, we try to choose a name that is somehow linked to the Swazi name or the story behind the child's arrival.

For example; the name Nkosikhona means "God with us," so we added the English name "Emmanuel" (God with us) to Nkosikhona's name. The first child to arrive at Project Canaan was named Melokuhle, but as he was the first child to enter "Canaan, the promised land," we added the English name Joshua to his name. In the Bible, Joshua was the first person to enter the land of Canaan after walking in the desert for 40 years with Moses.

Our Joshua is very proud to tell any new visitors that he was the first child to come here; it is very much a part of his identity. Rose and Gabriel are proud that they are the oldest children on Project Canaan (they didn't arrive as newborns) and are often given privileges enjoyed by first-born children. Our children all share clothes until they enter first grade. There is no doubt that some have favorite pieces, even as 2-year-olds, and wear them until they are threadbare, but once they are in first grade, they get to have their own clothes, which only they wear. This also helps with identity because they get to choose what they wear, it shows their personal style and how they want to be seen. It's cute to see who are the girly-girls who always want to wear dresses or the color pink.

Then there are boys who only wear t-shirts and others who always want to wear a shirt that has been buttoned to the top.

Birthdays are not a big deal in much of Africa, mostly because there wasn't a way to keep track of birthdays in the old days. You might ask an old woman when she was born and she would tell you that it was in the year of the big winds or give you an approximate age, but many Swazis don't know when they were born. Recently, when we were doing "well-child checks" on the children we feed through our church partners, many (if not most) of the children did not know their birthday or age.

We believe that celebrating birthdays is important and another way to build a child's confidence and help them with their identity. I love how the Aunties and Uncles take great pride in dressing each birthday child in brand-new clothes and shoes; they make sure hair is perfect and the child's face is shiny clean for the big celebration. Every child gets a birthday cake on his or her birthday and gets to share it with the children in that particular house of 40 children. We don't start giving birthday gifts until a child turns 3; that first gift is a big stuffed animal that they can proudly go and put on their bed. Each birthday has its own prescribed gift, but with a bit of a twist. For example, our birthday gift for age 4 is a book bag (backpack) since those kids are going to school. Still, each book bag is unique. Their fifth birthday is a handmade quilt, some coming from friends in Nova Scotia, Canada, and others from Georgia in the U.S. Each quilt is unique and that is the age when our children start to make their own beds and want to have them look very nice. We want them to take pride in their things and take good care of them.

The sixth birthday is a really big deal because it is an experience, not a thing. When a child turns 6, he or she receives a certificate that promises a game drive to see lions, elephants, giraffes, and other African animals. We typically wait for short-term volunteers to come and visit and then a group of children will go together with the visitors. It is such a fun day for all. The seventh birthday gift is a Bible and chocolate bar; the eighth birthday gift is a journal and a good water bottle filled with candy— which can be shared or not. Life lessons are learned with those candies, whether shared or not. The ninth birthday gift is a unique boy or girl devotional and, again, some candy that can be shared or not. Each year we will continue to have a fun, age-appropriate item or experience for our children to enjoy as we celebrate their lives.

When I was a child, we had a measuring stick behind the door at our cabin in Northern Ontario. Every summer, my cousins and I would line up to be measured, with everyone *ooh*ing and *aah*ing at how much each child had grown (or not). It was a fun family activity and rite of passage each year. As soon as we opened the Emseni campus, I wanted to start measuring our children, but couldn't figure out how to do it without making a mess on the walls. I thought about it for a year, while the children were still small, and finally one day I told Ian about my quandary. How and where could we measure hundreds of children, for many years, without it looking terrible? Ian thought about the question for a minute and then suggested that we build a boma (a beautiful African fence made of tall poles that touch each other to create a wall) and each child could choose their own boma stick upon which to record his or her measurement. We would write their name on their stick and each year measure them to celebrate how much they have grown. What a brilliant idea! (I really should ask him sooner for these ideas.)

Now, each child who lives at the Emseni campus (mostly 3 years and up) get to choose a growth stick and be measured on it each birthday. In addition, the birthday boy or girl gets to choose one special friend to go and watch the measurement ceremony, then sit in a place of honor and enjoy an extra-large piece of birthday cake. It is so fun to see who each child chooses, whether it is someone who petitioned all day or a child with whom they've been close since they were both babies. Sometimes a staff member gets chosen and with others, it is a biological sibling who is always present for a birthday party no matter where they live on campus. We want our biological siblings to bond and know each other as well as possible.

From an organizational perspective, we're intentional in preserving each personal history through a physical memory box and a virtual Dropbox. Here is how our system works: As soon as a new child arrives, we send an email to our U.S. office, with the name, birthdate, and all of the personal details of that child's life, including HIV status, medical history, and family history, when available. Much of this information would never be shared publicly, as it is very private and personal, but also a very important history to have if or when the child wants to know individual details.

As soon as the U.S. office gets this information, a Dropbox file is opened in the child's name and two sub-files are opened to include documents and photos. The document file is where we keep electronic copies of all legal documents including health card, Social Welfare report, court order, travel documents, others. The photo file also has annual sub-files. If a child arrived in 2014, there would be a photo file labeled "2014" and all photos of that child would be saved in that file. The following year a new file is opened for every child. We work diligently to take two photos a year of each child (Christmas and mid-year) to go in their file, along with birthday images. In this way, it is very easy for us to look back at the progress each child has made; when they turn 18, it will be very easy for us to print a book of photos of their life. The other good thing about this organizational system is that it doesn't depend upon me or anyone else remembering the details of their stories (which is impossible) or having photos on a personal computer, never to be found when needed. A very big family requires a very big, yet simple, system of organization.

In Eswatini, each new arrival receives a memory box, where we immediately wash and store anything that arrived with the baby, whether it's a blanket, clothing, hat, or other items. Even if we take clothing to the hospital to bring the baby home, we will then wash and put those clothes in the memory box. Not much goes into the box after that until the child starts school. Then we are intentional about choosing a piece of art or project that every child did that year in school and putting that in each box. It is labor-intensive and a labor of love. I know Spencer and Chloe loved (still do) looking back at old photos, baby clothes, or something from their childhood. It helps with grounding, history, and identity. The baby clothes will help with the eventual "where did I come from?" questions.

Each Sunday after a new baby arrives, we dedicate that baby to the Lord at church. Ian and I, as dad and mom, stand at the front of the church, present the baby to the older children and have them welcome the new baby by name. Then, I usually say something that reminds them all that they were once that tiny; I often name a child or two and tell them that they were little and cute like this new one, which gives everyone a chuckle, especially if I name one of the Aunties, Uncles, or even Ian. The thought of Ian being a small baby brings down the house with laughter.

As we pray for the baby, we also say specifically that this child was chosen to be placed in our family and that God has brought him or her to Project Canaan for a purpose greater than anything we can imagine. We can see the older kid's heads spinning and often get questions after church about where they came from or who brought them to Project Canaan. As they are still young, we have some standard answers that we all use, such as "Social Welfare brought you here." (That's a good catch-all, because they don't really know what that means, but they all get the same answer.) We may also say, "We will explain that more when you are older." (That's tried and true for all generations.) Each child will have access to their memory box when it is age-appropriate; we don't have to cross that bridge, yet.

Part of our identity comes from the understanding of "where do I come from?" That question can only be answered by talking about sex. This is an area of my personal life that I feel we failed as parents with Spencer and Chloe, so I was committed to doing that differently with the next few hundred children. It was just unclear about how and when to have that conversation. In most cultures, adults don't want to talk to kids about sex. Let's face it, it's uncomfortable, awkward, and can be embarrassing to everyone—but it is really important.

One day the senior supervisor, who is responsible for all of our children on antiretroviral (ARV) medication to manage and control their HIV status, came to me and shared some news from the doctor at the Baylor Pediatric AIDS clinic (Baylor). That's the clinic where our children receive their HIV treatment. She was told by the doctor that there are certain ages where it is important to start talking to children about being HIV positive.

Her reaction was similar to mine. *What?* Nope. Surely we can't do that!

The doctor explained that at some point in every HIV+ teen's life, they decide to stop taking their ARVs, which is disastrous. Once a person starts taking medication, it is critical that they continue to take it regularly. If they stop, the virus starts to work even harder against the body and the person will die.

Baylor struggles daily with teenagers and children who don't want to take their medication, hide it, spit it out, or simply refuse it and their viral load starts to increase, again. That is why the doctor brought it to our attention and further explained that, at the age of 8, we must sit down and have the first conversation about what HIV is, why they are taking medication, and why it is so important. At the age of 10, they need to know how HIV is contracted, be told how they got the virus (which, in our cases, would be from their mothers and that brings its own counseling issues), and how to prevent contracting the virus. *Yikes*.

I can't begin to think about how these conversations happen in Swazi culture, but I was much more concerned about the fact that Ian and I, as dad and mom, had to sit our HIV+ children down and tell them that they had a deadly virus. I knew I had until the end of 2019 to approach the subject before some of our children turned 9, and so, I put it on a shelf and left it there, untouched, until the time came. For that whole year, I thought it was us who had to actually say the words and explain the situation, but as the time drew near and I sought counsel on how we could possibly live through this conversation, I was told that the nurses at Baylor would do the talking, with flip-chart images. We just had to be moral support.

Wow! We'd dodged that bullet, but I was still sick to my stomach about the whole conversation having to occur. No child should have to learn about

HIV at the age of 8 and then be told that they have the virus. However, this is a part of their identity and how we handle the information, and how they handle their health will impact their lives.

A plan was made and the day for the first "conversation" arrived. Ian and I drove with two senior supervisors and two 8-year-old children to Baylor. My only goal for the day was to not cry (or vomit) in front of the children. In the end, the nurse at Baylor was so good at doing her job and explained everything so well that all the adults present survived and the children left feeling informed. They also seemed to feel safe in the knowledge that we were there with them and love them. Perhaps above all, they knew they were going to go to KFC for lunch when we were finished, so how big of a deal could this really be? I will tell you that the KFC that day was the most delicious I'd ever eaten in my whole life and I was beyond thankful that the conversation went well. There were no tears and no puking.

Having said that, there was one thing said during the flip-chart session that did derail us for a bit. The nurse told the children that they got the deadly virus from their mother. They both looked at me, asking in their minds, "Why would she give us a deadly virus?" I quickly spoke up and said that I was not the mother who gave it to them, but that opened up a bigger can of worms. What "other mother" do they have who would do such a thing and where is she? *Oh boy*. Now we had to really move the "sex talk" up the "to do" list and quickly, lest they start spreading the word that I was giving children a deadly virus!

I spoke with my friend and long-term volunteer Shelly Harp about my plight and she suggested that I read a book series called *God's Design for Sex* by Stan and Brenna Jones. It is a four-book series that starts that "conversation" with the first book. It is called *The Story of Me: Babies, Bodies and a Very Good God* and is written for children that are 3 to 5 years old. Age 3-5 seemed awfully young to me to be addressing the issue of where babies come from, but then again, if we start talking about it when they are that young, then it's not a big deal. There is no snickering, no laughing, or covering their eyes. It just is what it is. I thought maybe that could work for us.

I remember when two of the boys saw Nurse Hannah very pregnant with her second child. They asked her what happened to her stomach and she told them there was a baby inside. Both boys' eyes got as big as saucers and one of them asked, "Did you eat the baby?" Inquiring minds want to know!

The second book in the series is called *Before I was Born: God Knew My Name* and it is written for ages 5 to 8, so we started with that one in order to waylay any child-spread rumors that I am out to cause bodily harm to any of our children; it would help with introducing a basic understanding of how babies get inside their mother's tummy. (You readers with young children will be thanking me for this!)

As the book describes, it provides "a tactful but direct explanation of sexual intercourse between a husband and wife." First, I had to sit with my senior supervisors and explain my plan. Needless to say, I was met with big, wide eyes, faces buried in their arms, and shaking heads. We all wanted to die, but we also all knew it was an important conversation that none of them had ever had—with anyone. Many of them also have children at home and were not planning on addressing the sex issue. There is no sex education in school, so everyone is figuring it out on their own, leading to so many teen pregnancies, STDs, and HIV/AIDS.

After lots of blushing, eye-rolling, laughter, and questions, I left my team to make a plan that would work for them. They came back to me a week later with a wonderfully thought-out plan of action. The staff from the oldest girl's house (E5) and the staff from the oldest boy's house (E4) would take the girls and boys, separately, down to our Swazi homestead, have a fun day, prepare some fun food, and then sit on the grass mats to read the book. They planned to discuss body parts and we all wanted the children to know them in both English and siSwati, so it was decided that Ian and I didn't need to be there. *(Whew!)* It would just be more comfortable for everyone if we weren't. *No kidding!*

Two days later, the book had been read, the conversations had, questions asked and answered, and it was time for my peeps to come and give me an update. I have to tell you that I laughed until I cried at some of the things that were said. The children all think of me as "Mom," so when they learned that "mom" has a baby in her tummy for nine months and then the baby comes out, one of the girls said, "That's a lie!" When asked why she thought it was a lie, she answered, "Because some Sundays at church, Make Janine has two new babies and then the next Sunday she might have two more." Oops. We often introduce more than one baby on a Sunday. She was right to question how I could possibly do that!

Then there was the boy who came up to me and asked where his real mom was. One of the boys beside him told him that I was his real mom, but he said, "No, she's my fake mom." *Ouch.* We all knew what he was asking and I answered honestly that I did not know. He seemed satisfied with that answer and skipped away.

The next day, all of those boys and girls were in a van, heading to swimming lessons. One of our supervisors asked them to share something that they'd learned during their homestead visit the day before. Without missing a beat, one of the boys raised his hand to answer the question and blurted out, "Boys have two holes and girls have three." None of the kids reacted or laughed because he was just stating a fact. *All* of the staff cracked up when this was reported back to us.

We have started the ball rolling. Our younger children have now been taken through the first book and, again, it was no big deal—just another storybook, which should make conversations less awkward as the children grow. I will say that all of our staff felt very appreciative of the books and they were passed around the entire campus, with many people learning things about human reproduction and sex that they'd never known. One of my supervisors said that these books are quite possibly the most important piece of information that Project Canaan has ever shared with the Swazi people.

Lehora lekufundza means "knowledge is power." (Remember my chapter on education?) We want to empower our staff with knowledge and then they are in a better position to empower our children. If our staff knows who they are and their origin, then they can help our children understand who they are and how to embrace their own identity—not an identity inflicted by someone else. I believe that we are making progress.

We are raising Swazi children and they must identify as Swazi, so we are also intentional in this area. Language is the first and most important part of that identity. If they cannot speak, read, and write siSwati as well as another Swazi high school graduate, then we have failed, so we encourage siSwati to be spoken in the homes at all times. The children get enough English outside the home and at school. We also try to address the whole issue of our children living in dormitory-style homes, with communal kitchens for many children. That is so different from living in a homestead where the father has his hut, each wife has her own, the girls live in one, the boys live in another, and the gogo's house is at the center of it all, besides the kitchen. While we are not raising these children to leave us and go to live in a mud hut, the traditional Swazi homestead is an important part of the history of the nation and people. It is still how most Swazis live today, so we decided to build our own on the farm.

Our staff got so very excited about this; we see it as having our own Swazi Cultural Village on the property. We started with the gogo's house and the kitchen, then we built the kraal where outdoor cooking happens, bonfires, storytelling, and important conversations—about things like sex, life, love, and hope for their future. We are making some cultural adaptations, like both boys and girls learning how to prepare and cook food—girls aren't the only ones who work. We are sticking to the authenticity of not having running water or electricity, which caused quite a ruckus when the kids first went down and couldn't find the light switch, the ceiling fan, or the TV. They asked how they could possibly enjoy the time there without a TV. Our staff all laughed and told them that not one of our staff grew up with a TV at home and most didn't have running water or electricity.

There is a lot for our children to learn about their identity as Swazis and the Swazi homestead is a big part of that journey toward enlightenment. I've been reading Charles Martin's new book called *"The Water Keeper."* In it, he talks about the two questions that people need an answer in order to understand their own identity. The first is "Who am I?" and the second is "Whose am I?" He wrote, "In my strange line of work, I'd discovered that we as people can't answer the first until someone else answers the second. It's a function of design. Belonging comes before identity. Ownership births purpose. Someone speaks whose we are and out of that we become who we are. It's just the way the heart works."

I found that statement fascinating and read it just as I was writing this chapter. Coincidence? I don't think so. I believe that our children know they belong to our big family and the bigger family of God. I also believe that they know to whom they belong because we talk about their heavenly Father all the time. Ian and I might serve as parents on earth, but we will fail them and they must know that they are a part of the family of God. Only then will they be able to answer "Who am I?"

As I was writing this chapter, I was prompted to speak with a young Auntie named Nothando (pronounced *"non-tawn-doe"*), who lives with our girls at the Emseni Campus. She came to Project Canaan as a very broken, scared girl, who didn't belong anywhere. Nothando had no home and had been told by her very own family that she didn't belong to them. In fact, her story is much worse than that. When she was only 5, her mother left her and her 2-year-old brother with their father, then went on to live a life filled with alcohol, bad men, and bad choices. Eventually, she was poisoned by a jealous woman. Nothando's father brought in a new woman, but that woman never wanted Nothando and meant her harm. Both father and stepmother would go to work and stay away for weeks at a time, leaving the two young children alone. Nothando was always begging neighbors for food and scrounging through the forest, looking for wild fruit. There was nothing in her one-room house to eat and they were starving.

One day, a man came to her and told her that he would take her and buy her some food. He took her by the hand and led her into the bush, where he stopped at a tree, took off her clothes, and raped her. She remembers looking up at the tree, not knowing what was happening, feeling afraid. There was no food, only pain. The same man repeated this daily for months, except when her father was home. She had no one to tell and wouldn't have even known what to say.

One day, her father came home and told her that the stepmother didn't want the children living in the house anymore, so he took both children to their maternal grandmother. She lived in a large homestead, making traditional home brew for a living, and serving it at her shabeen that catered to drunk men. She herself was drunk most of the time and she was a nasty drunk, regularly beating Nothando and her brother. Home brew can be very dangerous because it's made with whatever is available and can lead to mental decay and even death. I remember once seeing a batch of home brew that had a car battery simmering *in* the liquid!

Their new home had two bedrooms and a sitting room. The first bedroom had a bed where the grandmother slept and a grass mat beside the bed on the floor where the two children slept. The second room was the bedroom of an old man. Nothando was unsure who he was, but he was very, very old. When the grandmother would go to town or to the forest to find ingredients, she would lock the children in the two-bedroom house with the old man. Not long after they arrived, Grandmother went away for a few nights. The old man asked Nothando to come and sleep in his bed to keep him warm. She did as instructed and the first night she awoke to the man taking off her clothes and raping her. That happened night after night to this sweet, innocent child of God and no one except the old man knew. On the nights that the grandmother was at home, both kids would sleep on the floor on a straw mat beside her bed. There were many nights that her drinking establishment patrons would pay extra for sex and the grandmother would lead the men into her bedroom and fulfill their every need, with the young children lying on the floor beside her, pretending to be asleep.

One afternoon, Nothando was playing around the back of her grandmother's house, which was also the shabeen, and in broad daylight, a drunken and mentally disturbed patron grabbed Nothando, threw her to the ground, pulled off her pants, and started raping her. The next thing Nothando saw was her grandmother running toward the man with a huge piece of wood and crushing the side of his head, knocking him off the tiny girl. Then she proceeded to beat him until others came and pulled her away.

It was only then that Nothando knew that what these men had been doing to her for so long was wrong. Her grandmother dragged her to the river to bathe her private areas and clean her up. She didn't take the child to a clinic or hospital, there was no treatment given and it was never talked about, again. It was many years later that Nothando discovered that one of these men had infected her with HIV. She was devastated, ashamed, and confused. From the time of the last assault until adulthood, she avoided boys and men. Even when she had a potential boyfriend, she did not want to be touched and the friendship would end abruptly. She believed that she was damaged goods, unworthy of love and unlovable.

She did not believe in God, because how could a good God allow such bad things to happen? Why wouldn't a good God protect an innocent child? Nothando got very sick and, while getting her HIV medication, she learned that she also had tuberculosis (TB). It wasn't "just" TB; it was multiple-drug-resistant TB and she landed in the National TB hospital in

Eswatini. It was there that she met a young woman, who had been in and out of that hospital, fighting for her life and her name was Nomsa.

Nomsa saved Nothando's life.

I first met Nomsa on the side of the road in the industrial town of Matsapha. She was sitting in the back of an ambulance, wearing a mask, holding her tiny twin baby girls. She was emaciated and being taken to the TB hospital, where she was not expected to live. A local Community Health Motivator (CHM) had found Nomsa lying on the floor of her mud hut, with her two newborn baby girls lying beside her. She was too weak to walk, get water, or to make breast milk for them to drink. Social Welfare called me to ask if the twins could be placed at the El Roi baby home and I said yes. I met them on the side of the road and took the babies from her arms, took a photo for their memory box, and said goodbye. Nomsa would eventually succumb to the horrific disease, but not before helping to save many lives.

I was convinced that if I visited Nomsa every week, took her healthy food, and brought her photos of her girls that she could beat the disease; she could then come and take her children back and raise them. She was so young and they were her fourth and fifth-born (second set of twins), but none of her children lived with her. Her lifestyle made that impossible. Nomsa did get stronger in the hospital and, over a period of 18 months, she became an advocate for women who needed one, often roping me into the process. Together we were able to rescue and provide a home for two other children and helped provide critical assistance to many other women who were suffering. One day she called me and told me that the women in her ward were asking for Bibles, so I delivered them—some in English, some in siSwati.

It was during my interview with Nothando, for this book, that I first learned she was one of the women who'd asked for a Bible. While she didn't believe in God, Nomsa kept telling her that God loved her and that if she would only read the Bible, she would know for herself that she can be forgiven and loved. Nomsa had gone through a lot of her own hardships in life after her mother had died when she was young, and she had much from which to be released once she asked for forgiveness. She was free and wanted that for her friend Nothando. Nomsa talked about Project Canaan often and actually came and lived in a socially isolated room on the farm during her time of hospice, so she could be loved near her girls.

After Nomsa died, Nothando contacted another friend who lived here and asked for a job. That is how she came to us. She was broken, hurting, and looking for a friend. She had hoped that Project Canaan would bring her a fresh start, a new beginning, and a place to put her feet down and forget about her past. One day, Nothando decided to share the story of her childhood with one of the women here, whom she thought she could trust, only to be betrayed, again, this time by a friend. As rumors started to spread about her life, she slid deeper into a pit of darkness and shame.

Meanwhile, Shelly Harp moved to Project Canaan, with her husband Barry and three of their boys to be long-term volunteers. When she saw the hurt in the hearts of so many of our Swazi women, she started focusing on women's ministry. We built a very special housing complex on the land that encompasses 13 single rooms, a common kitchen, toilets, and showers. It is designed exclusively for young women who have nowhere else to live. They may have been kicked out of their homestead, are living on the street, are pregnant and have nowhere to go, or are simply in desperate need of a home for themselves (and, often, their children). We designed and built these rooms and called them the "Sicalo Lesisha Kibbutz." Sicalo lesisha means *"new beginnings"* in siSwati and a Kibbutz is a collective community found in Israel, typically established based on agricultural development. Our hope was that by bringing needy women from a similar background together that they could find healing, redemption, and hope.

That is where Shelly met Nothando. Over many weeks that led to months, the women at the kibbutz gathered together for prayer, Bible study, friendship, and hard conversations. They talked about everything from how gossip can destroy a person to the importance of trust. They cried about rape, incest, and childhood trauma and laughed about "giving your pearls to pigs" (one of Shelly's favorite scriptures). Shelly became a friend, a mother, a sister, a pastor, and a priest to these young women, not the least of whom was Nothando.

One day, I noticed that Nothando was getting thinner (which seemed an impossibility, based on her tiny structure) and her big beautiful smile had gone dark. I asked Shelly about her and she shared that Nothando was really struggling with the shame of her past. She needed help. I could see that what Nothando needed most was love and there was a whole lotta love at Emseni 1 where our 3-year-olds live, so I moved her from her job at Khutsala to be a live-in Auntie for these little ones.

I had a few thoughts: First, she would be well fed by our kitchen, so she would put on some much-needed weight. Second, she had such a loving personality and our toddlers are so filled with the joy of life that they could provide love for one another. Lastly, in the safety of one of our children's homes, perhaps Nothando could be childlike herself and enjoy playing childhood games, singing silly songs, and building healthy relationships from the ground up.

She was afraid at first, but seemed to settle in well, getting to know the children's names (a daunting task for a newbie), learning how to fit in with staff, and even singing in the choir. One Sunday, though, I noticed her wrists bandaged while she was on stage at church. *Oh no.* Was she cutting herself? I grabbed Shelly after church and she pulled Nothando aside and asked her directly. Her answer was yes. She used to cut her legs, so no one could see it, but had recently started cutting her wrists. She explained that for many years she had struggled with sleep because her mind would always go back to the traumas of her childhood. She didn't want to close her eyes for fear of a bad dream, bad memories, and hands that grope in the night. She started taking pills, any kind of pills, hoping they would make her groggy. When that didn't work, she started cutting herself because the physical pain would distract her from the emotional pain that she felt in her very core.

There was a young man working on Project Canaan who took note of this beautiful young woman, and, one night, the Lord showed him her face in a dream. The Lord told the young man to go and speak to her and tell her that she was special and that God had something special prepared for her. He asked if they could get to know each other as boyfriend and girlfriend; she refused. She told him that she was not the type of girl that he wanted and even shared her HIV status to scare him away. She told him that she did not trust men and did not want to be touched by a man. Still, he was undeterred. He told her that the Lord had instructed him to pursue her and that he was to take care of her.

Shelly started meeting with the ladies in June 2017 and Nothando was hungry for the word of God. She wanted to be free from her past, free from her pain, and free from the bondage she had known so long. Shelly made a journal entry on August 9, 2017, that said, *"I noticed something special about her (Nothando) the moment I met her. She listened intently as I read God's word and taught the scriptures. I could see the Holy Spirit visibly moving her heart each time we met. She asked for prayer the second study and I could see she wanted Jesus, but did not believe He could want her. Her past was holding her back. Every week I could see the word of God knock the chains off her broken heart and healing taking place. Today I preached on baptism and she asked to be baptized!!! God is so good!"*

Later that month Nothando was baptized in the small swimming pool at the El Roi baby home. Today she is free. She is a beautiful, strong young African woman, who knows that God has a plan for her life and she believes that her past will allow her to minister to other women who have been through similar trauma. A few months ago, Nothando and her boyfriend came to speak with Ian and me; they told us of their desire to marry and to remain pure until marriage. They wanted to start their lives together in a godly way. In November 2020, we attended Nothando's wedding and couldn't be happier for this young couple.

Nothando is secure and confident and has found her identity in Christ. She is confident in whose she is and who she is. I can't wait to see what the Lord has planned for this young Swazi couple in the future. I know that her experience and freedom will help many young girls find true identity in the years to come.

CHAPTER SEVEN

Healthcare is Free; You Just Have to Pay for It

We have an expression that we use a lot: "We don't know what we don't know." I grew up in a home with both parents being pharmacists; we lived in an apartment on top of the drugstore. In fact, I come from generations of pharmacists and therefore feel some hereditary value in the medical field. From the time I could walk, I worked in the drug store facing up shelves. Eventually, I was tall and old enough to work in the dispensary, learning what various medications did or didn't do and what could happen if certain drugs were taken together. I heard many happy (but mostly sad) health stories that customers told my parents over the dispensary counter. My mom worked at the hospital pharmacy for a time, so I spent time there with her, too.

My point is that I assume everyone knows what I know; I don't know what other people don't know.

I remember Anthony Musyoka (one of the young Kenyans who came to Project Canaan at the very start) explaining to me several years ago how most Africans approach the issue of health. Anthony is now a Registered Nurse, having gotten his degree during his time with us at Project Canaan. While his explanation might not fit our western definitions, it was very eye-opening and enlightening. He explained that Primary Health Care is when people proactively go to the doctor, look after themselves, and are quick to seek help if they are sick or injured. Secondary Health Care is when patients go to the hospital or seek medical care after they have been sick for some time or have an open wound that has not healed in the time they hoped it would. He went on to explain that most Africans (yes, I realize this is a big sweeping statement, but it was made by an African, not me) rely on Tertiary Health Care. He gave an example of a person hit by a car, sustaining an open wound. The Tertiary Health Care approach would be to wait until it is festering and perhaps gangrene is setting in before they go to the hospital.

That made no sense to me since my experience growing up was in Canada, but now that I have lived in Africa for more than eight years and worked in many countries in Africa for 15+ years, I almost understand it. For example, just today, before sitting down to write, I was dealing with a staff member who had narcolepsy. I needed her in a very specialized capacity, so sent her to our own doctor for assessment and help. After a short conversation, she lay down to be examined and the doctor and nurse immediately saw a *huge* growth protruding out of her abdomen. She had complained of pain and severe bleeding for *six* years, going to many different hospitals to get help, but each time she was put on a drip (what they call an IV here), given some "tablets" (patients are not allowed to ask what they are or their purpose), and sent home. She'd assumed she had been treated and that soon she would be well. Only two months ago, she went with one of our supervisors, who made sure she got an X-ray and CT scan and was assured that she was fine. After all that, today, our doctor saw a tumor in her the size of a 4-month-old fetus.

Keep in mind that every time this poor woman went to the hospital, she had to take at least one day off work. (There are no general practitioners for the general public here. Everyone goes to a hospital to see a doctor and waits in line for many hours or days.) She had to pay for transportation to and from work AND she had to pay every time she went to the hospital, only to be given fluids and probably a multi-vitamin and sent home. Her narcolepsy was a result of the giant tumor that was growing in her abdomen and cutting off the blood circulation! *Can you imagine this??* No wonder Africans don't want to go to the hospital for a cut or scrape or headache. It's just not worth it and costs way too much time and money.

In the very early days of Project Canaan, when they were just starting to clear the land by hand to plant the first crop, Anthony was one of the laborers clearing the land; this was years before he went to nursing school. There was a tall, strong and beautiful young woman who worked on the farm and she was pregnant with her fifth child, but still working hard in the hot African sun for 12 hours a day. One Friday, she went to her manager and told him that she was overdue and thought she should go to the local clinic. He agreed and off she went. When she got to the clinic they told her that she should go to the government hospital in town to be induced. She packed up her things, took public transportation, leaving her other four children with her aging mother, and headed to town. When she got to the public hospital, she was checked out by a nurse and told to go to the outdoor hallway so she could walk up and down the hall until the baby started to crown.

This is not unusual and I have been witness and friend to many young women who go to government hospitals to give birth alone. They never have a birthing partner (husband, boyfriend, mother, or sister) along to assist. They walk up and down the outside corridor until the baby is on his or her way out and then they go to an open room with between four and 10 beds lined up side by side. They're instructed by the nurses to take off their clothes, leave them on the floor beside the table, and get on the table. Then, they push until the baby comes out.

There are no drugs, no epidurals, no words of encouragement, and, if the women start to unravel in their pain and fear, the nurses often beat them over their heads and bodies to make them focus on delivering the baby. I have witnessed this myself and know *many* women who have experienced this in government hospitals. I once wrote a blog titled, *"Madam, you must step out of the delivery room. You are too soft."* I was told this because I was trying to calm down the teen mom who wanted to commit suicide rather than give birth to the baby. Once the baby is born the mother immediately puts her street clothes back on, the baby is wrapped in a cloth that reminds me of tent fabric that doesn't absorb or stain, and a nurse carries the baby while the mother walks down the hall to the post-delivery room. She will stay until the next morning and then go home to wash and care for the newborn baby.

In the case of the tall, beautiful pregnant mama from the farm, that Friday night, she walked up and down the outside hallway for hours until the nurses decided to induce her. They gave her a tablet and told her to go walk some more. After another hour, they gave her another tablet then, the baby started to come quickly. There were no doctors available and that poor sweet young mother of four children died on the delivery table; her baby also died.

In my layman's opinion, those were preventable deaths. Proper prenatal care and monitoring, along with proper labor and delivery standards would have saved two precious lives. Instead, an old woman was forced to raise four children orphaned by poor healthcare—not HIV/AIDS, tuberculosis, nor any of the other "major health issues" we commonly see here. My learning curve continues to be steep and I now realize that maternal health and early childhood mortality are "major health issues" in developing nations. We are certainly in that category.

We were living in Atlanta when we got the call about the deaths of these two souls and I was in shock and so very sad for the whole family. It was at that moment that I knew we had to build a medical clinic on Project Canaan where prenatal healthcare can be given, birth control can be available, and education on both readily accessible. It took several years, but we raised the funds and built the El Rofi (the Hebrew name for God, which means "God who heals") Medical and Dental Clinic. The old woman who was left to grieve and care for those four grandchildren sat in a place of honor at its opening, tears rolling down her face at the memory of her deceased daughter. Since that day, she has been employed at the baby home and spends her days putting tiny baby clothes on the laundry line, taking them off when they are dry, and folding them sweetly.

It was time to start making some headway with Primary Health Care education. We were in a position to provide honest medical information, not false information based upon false beliefs. (For example, it is believed that if you have sex with a virgin, you will be cured of HIV/AIDS. That is a very common belief here and in other parts of sub-Saharan Africa.) We could provide a diagnosis and the right medication or treatment for each patient. That is uncommon at government clinics and hospitals, which have been out of many medications for years due to lack of government funding. We could do all of this for a "reasonable" price that would attract all 300+ Project Canaan employees to *want* to use our clinic because it would save them taking a day off work, a trip to town, and an all-day wait at the hospital.

We opened our clinic and announced that the price would be slightly less than that of the government hospital to make the offer even more attractive. We would charge E20, rather than E25 charged at a local clinic ($1.30 vs. $1.60) to see a nurse. That includes all medications, which we have in stock and the hospitals don't. We had a really good deal, too, that if you had to go to the clinic more than twice in a month, we wouldn't charge you more than twice; so, for a chronic cough or discharge (sorry, I had to say that), you could keep going back for free!

Crickets.

Nada.

No one wanted to come to the clinic. We added basic public health information to our bi-weekly *Lehora Lekufundza* learning sessions and Anthony, who is loved and respected by all, made it a point to encourage women to come for birth control and both sexes to come for STD treatment, wound care, and general health counseling.

Still crickets.

After a few months, a few patients started to show up and we had an ever-growing number of injuries on duty (which added more topics to our bi-weekly *Lehora Lekufundza* learning sessions), but we could never quite crack the nut of moving them from choosing Tertiary Health Care until someone had an idea—an idea that I did not think was good as I believed it would have a lot of pushback from our employees. Rather than having them pay to go to the clinic, we would change their employment contracts to automatically deduct E25 ($1.50) each month from their paycheck to cover their medical care. So, as Ian perfectly stated, "They might as well go to our clinic because it's free; they just have to pay for it."

BINGO! *It worked!*

Yes, there was grumbling and groaning in the first few days, but then, people started showing up at the clinic. We were concerned that some might take advantage of "free healthcare," but that's not what happened. We saw patients arriving who really needed help, health advice, and an advocate (like in the case of the lady with the giant abdominal – all the basic care which they had never received in their lives from a clinic or hospital. *Woohoo!* Who would have guessed?

(I wanted to be sure to include this in the book because there might be people reading this who have worked on projects all over the world and can't crack the health education and care "nut." My advice would be to provide it, charge for it, and educate, educate, educate, then repeat. *It works!*)

Speaking of healthcare, let me take a moment to give a shout-out to the Baylor Pediatric AIDS clinics that are found in three locations around the country. They are directly associated with Baylor University in Texas and responsible for the lives of thousands of children who are on antiretroviral treatment. We currently have 18 children who are HIV+ and they depend upon the free medication from the Baylor Clinic.

Treatment for HIV has come a long way since we first started working here in 2015. In the early days only, people whose CD4 count was at 200 or less were put on treatment, and even then, many of them died. The CD4 count is like a snapshot of how well your immune system is functioning. When the CD4 count drops below 200, a person is diagnosed with AIDS. A normal range for CD4 cells is between 500 and 1,500.

That was a problem because infected people started to refuse treatment (the only possible way that they could survive) because they saw family members die once they started taking the antiretrovirals. While antiretroviral treatment is free (paid for mostly by the Global Fund) here in the country, it is a very antiquated medication. The very first treatment used in 1987 called AZT is still being here while countries in the west have much newer (and more expensive) medications. For more information about AZT, watch Matthew McConaughey in the movie *"Dallas Buyers Club"* where he plays a man infected with HIV that is any kind of cure in the early days before treatment.

Every month, we have to take our HIV+ children to the clinic where they are weighed, height measured, assessed for general health, and then medicine adherence checked. Every six months, blood is taken and their viral load is measured to see how they are responding to the treatment. If their viral load is undetectable (which most of ours are), they simply continue with their medication and lead healthy lives, taking life-saving medication every day at 7 a.m. and 7 p.m. without fail. In fact, people whose viral load is undetectable are also non-infectious—very encouraging for when our children get older and want to marry and have their own children.

We have a medication report that is found in each house. One senior staff administers the antiretroviral treatment and a more senior person stands and bears witness to the child getting the medication. Then, both staff members initial that medication report. This might sound tedious or that we are overdoing it, but I assure you that is not the case. Each month, we also have to take the liquid and tablets back to Baylor: they measure how much liquid is left and count how many tablets are left; then, they compare that to what we should actually have left. We need to be between 95 and 105 percent compliant or we get a strong reprimand from the Baylor staff. It took us several years to get a system in place so that we were always within range and compliant, but non-compliance equals death. It is said that a person is better to never start on ART than to start it and stop it. When you stop, you get sicker faster and death is certain. Non-compliance is a very big problem in Eswatini with both adults and children. There is still so much stigma around this disease that no one wants anyone else to know that they are HIV+. So they hide their medication and often forget to take it. Parents also don't want others to know their children are infected and they hide their medication or don't give it to them if others are around.

I distinctly remember a doctor at the Baylor Pediatric AIDS clinic telling me that there is so much non-compliance in the country—meaning that children aren't getting to the undetectable viral load status and remain sickly—that he would assume the medication isn't working at all *if* it weren't for our children. He said that because almost all of our children have reached the undetectable viral load status, he knows that the medication does work when taken properly and with a proper diet that includes protein. Most of the children in Eswatini do not have clocks to know when 7 a.m. and 7 p.m. is; also, they do not have refrigerators to keep the medicine cool or proper diets, including protein.

Another doctor at Baylor asked one of our senior staff if we could help our Project Canaan staff kids because many of them are sick due to noncompliance. With our protocols in place and a system that works, could we possibly help them understand the importance of compliance and perhaps even develop a buddy system to help them manage? The problem with that idea is one of confidentiality. Baylor is not allowed to disclose anyone's medical status and, when our nurse asks about a staff member's HIV status, they most often lie about it. We will not give up on this, but will continue to educate, disciple, and seek to reduce stigmas around sick people. Baylor has 3,000+ children on ARVs in 2020 in Eswatini and most are not managing the disease well.

As I am writing this chapter in March of 2020 and those paragraphs about Baylor, the Covid-19 has just appeared in South Africa (only two weeks after it arrived in the U.S.) and I received a phone call from one of their doctors. They asked us no to bring our children to their clinic but to keep them at home and away from potential disaster. *What?*

She went on to say that she couldn't understand why people were just going on with their lives like nothing was going to happen. She said everyone at Baylor is freaking out because the tsunami is coming: We can hear the wind, but we can't see the wave. I told her that I had some conversations with my senior staff this morning and asked why some people are very afraid of the virus, but most people don't seem to be worried. They explained that most Swazis think this is a "white's disease," since what they are seeing on TV is happening in China, Europe, and the U.S. They don't believe it will get to Eswatini. We have been watching the news in the U.S. religiously and see the empty shelves in stores and reports of toilet paper aisles being the first ones to empty. Here in Eswatini, they are not afraid of not having enough toilet paper because most Swazis are too poor to ever buy it, so it won't be missed. (They use leaves or crumpled up newspaper.) Most Swazis are too poor to have a pantry, so there is no stocking up on food. With 70 percent of the population being subsistence farmers, there is no money for stocking up.

Remember this is a people group currently living with the highest HIV/AIDS rate in the world and an estimated 70 percent of the population is living with active or inactive tuberculosis (according to a doctor at the National TB Hospital), so they are used to terrifying, life-taking illnesses.

What does make them afraid are the government hospitals because they have been out of critical medications for the past couple of years. How will they possibly be able to help really sick people if the situation worsens? There are no masks for hospital workers, there is no protective gear, and there are reports that some nurses just don't want to go near sick patients. There are only four functioning respirators in the entire government healthcare system in the country. I had a nurse say to me, "In the west, people who are thought to be sick with the Covid-19 are considered "people of interest." It is the opposite here in Eswatini—no one is interested in them." *Ouch.*

On March 17th, we knew that South Africa was beginning to close their borders to Eswatini, so Ian and I jumped in the car and made the five-hour drive to Pretoria. We spent the day going from one pharmacy to the next to get the medications that our children would need for the next eight weeks. We had to work quickly and only got 75 percent of what we needed. We haven't been able to get critical medications for many months from Swazi suppliers and someone always has to drive to South Africa to get medications each month. We pray that the borders will reopen before our medications run out. We also purchased eight weeks' worth of food and supplies for our 261 children and the 95 staff members who care for them.

It has been widely reported that we have only had one case of Covid-19, a woman who arrived from Germany, but we aren't sure whether testing is being done or reported accurately. Swazis are telling me they're afraid of not enough tests, dishonest reports, and no possible medical care if they do get sick—which they surely will.

We are all trying to practice social distancing, but Swazis (like most Africans) depend upon public transport or small vans crammed with as many passengers as will fit. If the thought of contracting tuberculosis wasn't terrifying enough, Covid-19 increases the risk and fear, but still, that transportation is the only way for them to get from A to B. There is also the old practice of "sharing a meal," which is common to most of the African continent of one billion people. Families share the same meal from the same bowl. We see it from the front office to Khutsala where two or three people will take turns cooking that week and bring a plastic bowl of food; everyone eats from that same bowl with their fingers.

The irony that I have spent a good part of this chapter and book talking about viruses, poor healthcare, and TB is not lost on me. The Covid-19 pandemic has just passed its sixth month on the planet (as far as we know). This new virus has arrived to threaten the Kingdom of Eswatini and nations all over the world. All of our borders closed while we were watching with shock as the pandemic moved from China to Europe to North America and down to Brazil. It seems to have now circled the globe and parts of the world are doing better than others. Our friends in Taiwan have behaved beautifully and seem to have the virus under control. Schools will go back as planned and relatively few lives have been lost. South Africa closed its borders to all neighbors in March, and as we are land-locked, we are stuck. There have been a few repatriation flights to the U.S, but otherwise, no one is going anywhere.

As time passed, fear of this virus started to grow among the Swazis because neither the high-rate HIV nor the prevalent tuberculosis is even on the WHO or CDC lists of "underlying conditions." Also, I haven't mentioned the very high prevalence of hypertension or asthma among Swazis because I was telling you about higher risk, transmittable diseases. What was down is up and what was up is now down. What I will say is that Swazis are now terrified of Covid-19 due to their underlying conditions that include *all* of the above. Our healthcare system is already broken and, often, there is no basic medication even for hypertension or asthma. You can imagine what healthcare will look like with Covid-19.

On March 25th, Eswatini shut down. We typically follow South Africa's lead on these types of guidelines and we became a police state with travel only permitted with an official letter — even to go to the grocery store. We are now 150 days into lockdown and the new infection rates in South Africa are starting to soar.

Just after the lockdown started, I was approached by a young man who works at Project Canaan. He had a large lump on his neck and was sent to the government hospital for testing. The surgeon removed a small growth the size of a walnut in its shell. They explained to him that there were more of those growths in his throat, but before removing them, they must send the sample away for testing to see if it was cancerous. Then, they explained that they couldn't send the sample to their lab as the government hadn't paid the bill in so long, so the lab wasn't doing any more tests. The doctor handed the young man the sample bottle with the lump in it and sent him home, telling him to get it tested. He sent me a photo of the sample. (I get the WEIRDEST photos on my WhatsApp account!)

The young man did not have the $100 to pay for the test as that amount would be half of his monthly salary, but we had to know whether the growth was cancerous. So, I pulled funds from my Compassion Purse (donations made by people for random financial needs like this) and sent it off to one of the labs we use. The tumor was cancerous. It was Hodgkin's Lymphoma, a very treatable type of cancer—but not in Eswatini, not without access to private cancer care in South Africa at a considerable cost, and not at all with the borders closed.

He sits and waits, hoping for the best.

A few weeks later, I was approached by a young woman who had been having terrible abdominal pain for years. She had been in many hospitals around the country and the doctors kept telling her to just have a baby and everything would be fine. With my limited layperson knowledge of the human body, I assumed they were suggesting she had endometriosis and delivering a baby would clear it up (if she could get pregnant). She wasn't married, had had a rough childhood, and did not want to have a baby out of wedlock — that was not a viable option for her. As she described the pain and regularity, I got more concerned that this could be something else. I have a dear friend here who is a gynecologist and sees any of my girls for free; in fact, she has saved several of my Auntie's lives. When there is surgery (even emergency Cesarean section births), she never charges for her surgical time. We only pay, again from my Compassion Purse, what the hospital bills us. I sent the young woman to see this doctor and a few hours later I received a photo on my WhatsApp of the womb. It appeared that there was a large mass, which looked like an ectopic pregnancy; however, there was no fetus. This young woman wasn't ignoring her health or avoiding hospitals or doctors; she was just getting poor advice that might lead to her premature death.

This is the type of care that was being given *before* the Covid-19 virus hit Eswatini. Only God knows what is to come.

We have a young woman working on the children's campus as a new Auntie who went to our clinic for cervical and breast cancer screenings that we do a couple of times each year. I believe that this is one of the most important services that we provide at our clinic, and each screening reveals at least one woman who needs cancer treatment. Most don't receive it, some die at home, and some just disappear, but few, if any, get medical care for cancer. During this regular checkup, there were several lumps found on this young woman's breasts. When the nurse told the Auntie that she had lumps, some of them quite large, and needed to see a doctor, the Auntie responded that she knew about them as they'd been there for several years. When the nurse asked why she hadn't gotten help, the Auntie said that the last time she was at a government hospital, the nurse told her to go home, get her belongings, then come back so that they could cut her breasts off. I am not making this story up.

Now, years after this 23-year-old first found a small lump, more lumps have been found, and just last week, they found cancer in her cervix. This time, the hospital told her that the surgical ward is closed for renovation and no other hospitals are doing "elective surgery." Her breast and cervical cancer are not considered to be emergencies. The one and only cancer center in the country is closed; as a result there is no cancer care in Eswatini at this time and there is no way for her to get to South Africa for care.

Honestly, I'm struggling to write these last few paragraphs because we wrestle every day to keep our chins up, not be discouraged, and resist freaking out completely. We have to "keep it together" for so many others who are afraid and starting to get sick, but there are days that these stories are just too much.

Earlier this week, I received a call from a social worker who asked if I could go to the local police station and pick up a newborn baby just found in the bush, then take that baby and the police officer to the hospital. Why? Because the government cars have no fuel right now and the police had no way to take the baby for care, that's why they called Social Welfare to come and get the baby. Social Welfare doesn't have any fuel either, so they called us.

What about all the other babies or children who are in need around the country? Who will help them if the police or Social Welfare can't? I agreed to go to the police station and have Anthony assess the baby, then bring the baby here into quarantine rather than taking the newborn to a hospital that is at the epicenter of our Covid-19 cases to date. As I was speaking with the police officer, she was telling me about all of the young girls getting pregnant because they have been out of school for many months, with no sign of school reopening this year. Also, the prevalence of rape is up—in a country that already has a high incidence of rape. She warned me that there will be many, many more abandoned babies in the next six to nine months.

I don't know what Covid-19 is going to do to the Kingdom of Eswatini, the country of South Africa, or the continent of Africa, but we all fear the worst. There is very little we can do. We have increased our handwashing, sanitizing, and general bio-security, but it is impossible to keep this monster subdued. We have many people at Khutsala who are sick and quarantined at home, but they are unable to get a test because they just aren't available now. Private tests are sometimes available for $170, which is more than most Swazis make in a month.

I will say that everyone here is wearing a mask because they believe that a mask is the only other way to stay safe. As I write this, there is a huge controversy in the U.S. about mask-wearing and I don't know where this will land on the other side of history. But, from where I am sitting, it is heartbreaking to watch one of the most powerful countries in the world be the only one that is divided over whether or not to wear masks to save lives.

I don't know where the world will stand with Covid-19 by the time this book is published, but you will be able to watch for us in the news. They are saying that the world will not be safe until there is a vaccine. We can't even get chicken pox vaccines here in sub-Saharan Africa, so I can only imagine that we will be the last to get a Covid-19 vaccine. For now, our children are safe and we pray that the Lord will continue to protect us as we continue to serve Him. What I do know for sure is that Covid-19 is a part of the bridge to our children's future that I wasn't considering at the beginning of this chapter. Only God knows how much impact it will have on their lives.

CHAPTER EIGHT

Water Security: What's the Big Deal?

I could write another book about how many challenges we've had with people who feel we should not focus *all* of our efforts on "only helping a few dozen children," when the entire country is suffering. Others thought that it was selfish to raise $850,000 to become water secure on Project Canaan while the rest of the country desperately needed water. Why should we ask donors to invest in a project of this scope when so many people lacked clean drinking water?

As I have said before, it's important to focus or fail. The children are the heart of our work and the farm is the heartbeat. We can't keep one alive without the other. While food may equal life, you can't grow food without water—so, really, *water equals life.*

Sustainability is a buzzword widely in use by nonprofits all over the world and it is a word that we also use a lot. We are serious about it, focused on it, and intentionally running a sustainable farm. Some would say that this is impossible, or perhaps even laughable since the U.S.

federal government spends more than $20 billion a year on subsidies for farm businesses. About 39 percent of the nation's 2.1 million farms receive subsidies with the lion's share of the handouts going to the largest producers of corn, soybeans, wheat, cotton, and rice.[1] How does anyone make money, or even just not lose money, by farming? God has given us farmable land. He has given us mouths to feed and sent us people who need employment, so our farm had to become the epicenter of Project Canaan. In order to start farming, we needed water, and unfortunately, the land did not come with a river. In our early days, we had to depend upon seasonal rains, from November to early April, and we needed a dam to capture those rains.

We currently have three dams on Project Canaan. If you are thinking of pursuing sustainable farming, you won't want to skip this chapter.

Dam #1 was built in 2010 very shortly after the land was purchased. In fact, this was a small dam put in place by the former landowners to provide water for their livestock. That made it inexpensive and easy to expand so that we could irrigate 15 acres of crops. As we focused on expanding the fields, painstakingly ripping out the bush and removing rocks by hand, we realized that more water would be needed quickly and so a second dam location was found. In 2011, we built Dam #2, which allowed us to double our irrigated crops to 30 acres. We still didn't have enough capacity to irrigate the 80 acres, which was our goal, and a third, much larger dam had to be constructed. In 2012, we started the process of building Dam #3. It would take two years from the initial engineering plans until we broke ground to start building a water catchment that would eventually hold 12 million gallons of rainwater!

We weren't living in Eswatini when the first two dams were built, so we weren't directly involved in the construction. But how hard could it be? As I said in Chapter Four, *everything* is hard here, but I will also say that we have had fun learning, listening, growing, and being stretched well beyond our human capacity. Dam #3 was Ian's baby and he worked tirelessly to get it done.

The first thing required to build a new and much larger dam was to obtain an Environmental Management Plan (EMP). This plan had to be approved by the Eswatini Environment Authority and it would identify any problems that might arise as a result of the dam being built. How hard could that be? They wanted to make sure that if the dam breached, it would not flood other homes or farms downstream. They needed to confirm that we were not damming off a river that was providing water to other homesteads or farms. They wanted to be sure that we were not destroying protected species of trees, animals, or rare plant life. Ian likes puzzles and this project was a giant puzzle to him: from figuring out who in which department could do the survey to navigating Swazi government, politics, and culture as the new guy on the block. Thankfully, his cautious reserve, gentle nature, and persistence worked on his side even when his patience wore thin. But it paid off and, by the end of 2012, the EMP was approved and we were ready to get started. The next challenge was to raise the $332,000 needed for us to build the dam, the pump house, add the pumps and the piping, and buy the tools needed to irrigate the additional 50 acres. As I've now said numerous times, *how hard could that be?* Everyone knows the importance of water, so it should be a breeze to raise the funds, right? *Nope.*

Let me say something that might seem controversial or even harsh. No one really cares about water in the developed world because everyone takes water for granted. If you want water, just turn on your tap, right?

If you want to irrigate your fields, just turn on the hose pipe. Raising money for a dam was just not "sexy" and people to whom we spoke just weren't interested. However, we found one person and one organization that not only cared about water around the world, they also took action to provide water—and even more importantly, water security.

Lewis Lu is the "one" person. He is a mild-mannered librarian who works at the Changhua Senior High School (CSHS) in Changhua, Taiwan, and has been a dear friend for many years. Think "Superman" in a librarian's humble garb. Mr. Lu's passion for the country of Eswatini, his passion for teaching his students about helping the poor and his passion for supporting *Heart for Africa* drove him to be the first person to step forward and help us raise funds for this important project. Students from around the world joined students from CSHS and marched through the streets of cities throughout Taiwan shouting, "Walk for water!" in English and Chinese. Their efforts provided us with the seed money needed to get the ground cleared and prepared.

Rotary International is the "one" organization. This is an international service organization whose stated purpose is to bring together business and professional leaders in order to provide humanitarian service and to advance goodwill and peace around the world. Rotary International is comprised of more than 1.2 million members in 35,000 clubs globally. It cares deeply about water around the world and has raised hundreds of millions of dollars to help communities drill boreholes, provide safe drinking water, build toilets, and provide water at schools. Rotary has even developed a hygiene (WASH) education program. A direct quote from their website says, "Clean water, sanitation, and hygiene education are basic necessities for a healthy environment and a productive life.

When people have access to clean water and sanitation, waterborne diseases decrease, children stay healthier and attend school more regularly, and mothers can spend less time carrying water and more time helping their families." *Preach it,* Rotary International! They understood the problems and were already taking action, so we decided to approach a few of our Rotarian friends.

Some of you have perhaps been told that working with Rotary International to receive funding is challenging. It takes a long time and and is time-intensive. All of those statements are true, but believe me when I say that it is all worth it! Rotary International is a wonderful group of people committed to serving in their local communities all over the world. My father was a Rotarian, as was his father. Ian's father, Jim Maxwell, is a Rotarian, and in fact, the Rotary Club of West Ottawa was one of the first to help out on this project. *(Thanks, Jim!)* I have never met a Rotarian that I didn't like; they are kind, thoughtful, and engaged. I don't know how they do such a good job of making their brand work, but I have often said that if Christians were as consistent in their behavior as Rotarians are, we wouldn't have such a bad name.

Ian dug in and focused on what needed to be done. First, he contacted John Bach, who had traveled to Project Canaan with his wife PJ and was a huge *Heart for Africa* supporter. He was also the past President of the Rotary Club of North Fulton, in Alpharetta, Georgia (U.S.), a club of 30 Rotarians. Several years earlier John had established a relationship with the Rotary Club of Mbuluzi-Mbabane of Eswatini. Together, the two clubs developed a joint project, resulting in the donation of a John Deere Tractor to Project Canaan. When Ian brought the idea of a massive dam project to John, his initial reaction was that the idea was beyond the scope of the club's capacity. However, the then club President, Ben Hunter, liked the idea and began the process of applying for a Rotary International Foundation Global Grant. At that point, John was on board and became a passionate advocate in our pursuit of water security. He worked with Ben on the application process and helped us obtain the funds necessary to keep moving forward in our vision of sustainability. A Rotarian, who happened to be a dam engineer from Australia, was sent to Eswatini to help thoroughly assess the situation and help write the final grant application. We submitted the application and waited, with fingers and toes crossed!

In the end, seven Rotary Clubs in the U.S. and Canada partnered with the Mbuluzi-Mbabane Club to raise $50,000, which was then matched by the Georgia Rotary District matching funds (making it $100,000), which was matched again by the Rotary Foundation. This $200,000 grant was the single largest grant ever given by the District and one that we were very proud to receive. *Heart for Africa* was tasked with raising the balance of $132,000, and with the momentum from the Rotary International grant, Ian's drive to get the project done and the hand of Almighty God on the project, the funds were raised. As one of my Catholic friends in Taiwan always says, "If it's God's will, it's God's bill."

I want to pause to encourage any of you who are looking at a mountain that seems too high to climb, a river too wide to swim, or, as we say in Africa, an elephant that is too big to eat. As a follower of Jesus, I would strongly encourage you to pray for divine direction and make sure that what you are dreaming about is really from the Lord and not from a bad piece of meat you ate.

If there are lots of naysayers, then there's a good chance it's from the

Lord. If it seems an impossible dream, then there's a good chance it's from the Lord. If there is no way you could do this on your own, there's a good chance it's from the Lord.

He will use your skill sets, as well as the skills of others, as He did with Ian, Lewis Lu, John Bach, and others, but none of those people could have made this happen on their own. Then you must have patience (in siSwati "ooh-bay-gay-tay-la") and do things in *His* timing, not yours. While it took two full years for the vision of Dam #3 to become reality and for construction to begin, Ian was still busy with many other projects on the go. He didn't simply focus on this one thing with hopes to get it done quickly.

God's timing is always perfect. Over the last 15+ years, we have learned that He wants to invite many people into His story and that is why the stories that I share are robust and filled with awe and wonder—because He meant for them to be that way. Not only did this one project include people from the U.S., Canada, and Taiwan, it involved people from Israel, where we had to order the pumps for the pump house, and it involved people from Kenya, where we got the irrigation pipes. It even involved the government of Eswatini (Ministry of Works), who partnered with us to actually build the dam. The Swazi government is not known for being overly helpful or easy to work with, but the Ministry of Works was outstanding and became a long-term partner and friend to Project Canaan.

Construction of Dam #3 took six months to complete—a lot less time than it had taken to begin. The first step was to clear the African bush; then, to install a trench that ran perpendicular to the dam wall, centered with a safety drain at the dry end, all encased with rebar in concrete.

The Ministry of Works sent out two excavators, two dump trucks, one bulldozer, one grader, and one roller. We paid for the diesel and the equipment operators. They rented us the equipment at a reduced price, which helped us avoid having to raise even more money. While we were waiting for the heavy equipment to arrive, Ian searched for a supply of the clay that would be required for the waterside of the dam wall to make it waterproof. We thought we would need to truck that in from another location, but guess what? We found a large deposit of clay, only 500 yards from where the dam was being built. If it's God's will, why wouldn't He provide His own clay?

Once construction started, we saw dozens of loads of clay dug out of the ground, poured into a 10-cubic-yard dump truck, and driven over to the dam location where it would be dumped on the ground, only to then be graded level and packed down by the roller. This happened all day, every day, five days a week, throwing thousands of cubic yards of dust up into the blue sky with each trip. For four months, thousands of truckloads of clay were moved from one location to another, and in the end, we were able to build the whole dam with clay, not just the waterside. God doesn't do things half-baked. His plans are to be executed with excellence and to the best of our abilities while we get to watch and see what He does with *His* abilities.

Six months later, the dam was complete with walls that are 50 feet high and a basin that would fill with 12 million gallons of rainwater just five months later. We renamed Dam #3 the "Living Water Dam," and in December 2014, John Bach and members of the North Fulton Rotary Club were present as we dedicated the dam to the Lord. It was a glorious day. Little did we know that only 11 months later, the worst drought in sub-Saharan Africa would begin and the Living Water Dam would empty, once again becoming dry, cracked earth.

I'm already exhausted as I write this story, but wait until you hear what happened next.

In 2016, drought hit the land like a plague and it wasn't just Eswatini; it was all of sub-Saharan Africa, which includes 46 of the 54 countries that make up the continent of Africa. Rivers, the primary source of water for drinking, cooking, washing, and watering gardens dried up completely. Boreholes that once provided communities with (usually) safe drinking water were empty. Gardens were bare, fields were too hard to plow, and people started dying. While we thought that having three dams filled with water would be enough, we quickly realized that using any of that precious water to irrigate our fields would potentially leave us with no water to wash babies, cook, or flush toilets. Needless to say, that would be a disaster. As previously mentioned, all three of our dams are filled by rainfall, so when there was no rain to replace the water we use, the water in the dams disappeared, seemingly overnight. It was actually quite shocking to us all to see the water disappear and a decision to stop our entire agriculture program had to be made quickly.

Once the farm was "closed," Ian started working on how we were going to find enough water to live once the dams were empty. There is no aquifer (underground body of water) under our dams, so when the water was gone, it was gone. He reached out to several local water specialists, spoke with the Minister of Agriculture, and cried out to God for a solution. After all, only God can make it rain and only God can stop the rains from falling, so we needed His guidance again.

Before purchasing the land, Ian had first gone on a nine-hour journey through this piece of the African bush with the former landowner. They'd gone to the top of the mountain, where they climbed down a steep rocky crag to discover a waterfall. It was explained that the waterfall was connected to five natural springs coming up out of the mountain. As Ian prayed about a solution to our water problem, he was reminded of this active source of fresh water on the property. But how could we get the water from the springs down to the farm?

Ian put a call in to his new friend at the Ministry of Works and asked if he knew of anyone with expertise in hydrology who could help and the answer was "yes." Ian was introduced to a company called WaterWorx and the owner and co-founder, Gil Lanir, "just happened" to live on the other side of the top of our mountain. He was not only an Agricultural Engineering specialist from Israel, but he was also married to a Swazi woman and worked on water projects all over Eswatini and other parts of Africa. He was an avid hiker and knew the springs and waterfall well. In fact, Gil told Ian that he had recently been hiking in that area, and even in the midst of the drought, there was still water flowing. He was confident that this water source might be the solution to our problem. Ian and Gil sat down over a cup of coffee and worked on a plan to bring water from the top of the mountain to the farm.

The first thing that had to be done was a weir test, which measures the volume of water per hour that is flowing out of the streams. The test is done by damming up each stream and measuring the water coming through per hour. The tests were a success, with 2,200 gallons of water coming through each hour, even at the height of the drought. The next question was whether we could get the water to the farm using gravity.

While it looked like it was all downhill from the top, there were hilltops in between that went up, not down — we needed to learn if they were too high to push water over. Once they had that challenge solved, Ian wanted to know if we would have enough water pressure coming down the mountain to generate our own hydroelectric power. Electricity is very expensive here because most of it is imported from South Africa. It's also very unreliable, so we might go hours or days without electricity. Hydroelectric power would be a miraculous addition to our goal of becoming fully sustainable.

In the end, we learned that we would need a high-pressure pipe to be able to achieve that, and between the additional cost of the pipe, plus the generators that would be required to complete the project, we would need to raise close to $2 million for the project. Remember, we had just spent over two years raising the $320,000 needed for the Living Water Dam. Frankly, we were in a crisis—the most significant drought in recorded history—and we didn't have years to raise another $2 million, so we had to change the plan. In the end, the pipeline was redesigned to have pressure breaks along the way, reducing the cost by more than half to $850,000. That was still a mountain of money to raise to get water out of a mountaintop and the whole thing was daunting, but Ian never wavered. He knew that without water, the project could not continue. Without water, we would die.

He also knew that this was God's problem, not his. God put the water in the mountain for a reason and Ian believed that it was for us to use for His project.

We had a plan, we had a quote, and now we needed to present the idea to our Board of Directors for their approval and support. Remember what I said about water security at the beginning of this chapter? What's the big deal? Our presentation of the solution didn't quite go as we had expected. In Ian's words, here is what happened in the months to follow:

"The first presentation to the Board was thorough, but generated a lot of good questions, such as 'Can we put in more boreholes? Are we able to buy water in town and bring it out, rather than raising all that money? Have we ever built and maintained a pipeline before? Why would we waste money providing water for just us when the rest of the country is in need? Do you have water rights? Why don't we raise the money and put in boreholes all over the country?' Etc. etc. We responded by creating an FAQ document that provided responsed to all of the questions. We conducted water hydrology surveys to see if we could put in more boreholes, but found that the nation was struggling with finding water underground; boreholes were not being drilled because there was no water to be found. Questions from the Board became more repetitive, more aggressive, and more insistent, but our answers remained the same. The Board wanted new information or perhaps a different solution, but there was no new information because the questions had been answered. In a country where there was no water, God had presented us with a supply of water; we just had to bring it down the mountain.

In the end, the issue of whether or not to raise money to build a six-mile pipeline from the top of the mountain to provide water security for the entire property for now and the future caused division and dissension amongst our Board of Directors and a split that would bring disappointment and deep hurt. I was disappointed in how some Board members responded. They weren't living in Eswatini as we had been since 2012, and they can go to any number of their taps in their homes or places of work and turn them on, knowing that they will flow with never-ending, clean water. During a drought in the U.S., the grass on lawns might wither, but everyone can still take a shower every day. We didn't have that luxury and were uncertain how long we would be able to bathe our children. On the other hand, I was so thankful that other board members stepped up because they understood the importance of water security. They became vocal champions of the cause and pushed the project forward."

Eventually, the project was approved and a fundraising campaign was launched. His timing was perfect, again, as we had just hired David Bryant as our Chief Development Officer at *Heart for Africa*; and while he was quick to tell us that he wasn't a "rainmaker," he was also quick to show us how much he loved people and how much he loved inviting people into God's story. As the person primarily responsible for fundraising, David never feels as though he is asking people for money, but rather inviting them to invest in the Kingdom of God. We raised some initial funds, but the first significant donation that really moved the project forward was a $100,000 gift made by a newly married couple who felt God calling them to make a sacrificial gift from their 401K— and I mean *sacrificial*. Once again, we had confirmation and affirmation that we were moving in the right direction.

As we often do, we broke this mammoth project down into phases. Phase One included building roads to the springs, clearing more bush and building two dams to redirect the water toward a pipeline. Phase Two included building a one-mile steel pipeline, above ground and around the mountain, that would connect the two dams and take the pipe to the crest of the highest peak. Phase Three included building a three-mile OPVC pipeline that was buried underground and terminated at a 110,000-gallon water tank. Our friends from Rotary were able to redirect, with Rotary Foundation approval, the excess funds from the Rotary Foundation Global grant for the dam to be used to fund this tank.

Phase Four included building two miles of pipeline from that Rotary water tank to another 110,000-gallon water tank, which was also funded by Rotary through the "Kathy Myers Competitive Grant" (it was made possible through generous donations from Rotarian Kathy Myers before she passed away in 2012). In just two years, we raised $850,000 to fully fund this project. As we would finish one phase of the project, the Lord would "release" funds for the next phase. There were definitely glitches along the way, but the Lord was always with us.

What's a glitch, you ask? Well, the pipes we had planned to order were being made in South Africa and could be easily accessed and shipped. Once we had the funds to order the pipes, we learned that the new company in South Africa had not gotten their production up and running, so we were forced to order the pipes from their head office in Spain. Spain? *Yep.* Spain.

While sitting on our patio, writing this chapter together, I asked Ian to summarize how he felt about this whole project. He said, "It was a pig. Getting the materials to the top of the mountain (yards of gravel, sand, and cement) to the locations was almost impossible. Trucks couldn't go there, so everything had to be moved by hand. The Swazi men (wearing flip flops) were surfing down the side of the mountain with 200 pounds of wet cement in wheelbarrows to build the dams, dozens of times each day. These guys loved the challenge of doing something that seemed impossible and they rose to the challenge. I am so proud and thankful for them. This project showed me, once again, why I live in a state of awe at how our God works. He invites everybody to His table and the ones who say 'yes' get to see Him at work. It's fun to see it all unfold." That's my hubby.

I remember seeing what looked like a snake making its way across the fields from the bottom of the mountain toward the egg barn. I knew that it wasn't a giant snake, but rather the last bit of trenching being dug so that the final stages of the pipe could be laid. It was a beautiful sight from our patio. Finally, the day for which we had been waiting arrived. The pipe was connected to the water tank and all we had to do was to "turn on the tap," so to speak, or open the valve to let the water flow. We gathered our long-term volunteers, our older kids, and some of our staff to be there to celebrate the water pouring out of the pipe into the tank. So much heartache, so much stress, so much anger and so much division over the years, and yet there we stood, ready to celebrate. Ian had his drone camera up in the air, I had my iPhone ready to record a video and we did a countdown to open the valve!

Nothing happened.

There was no water, no nothing. Apparently, one of those pressure valves was closed higher up the mountain and not letting water through. We have a saying here that our family uses all the time and that is, "You have to learn to live with disappointment." That is a life lesson that Ian and I were both taught at a young age and one that we are teaching anyone who will listen. Trust me, work like this will teach you that lesson as well. Life is full of disappointments, but it's how you handle them that affects the outcome of that disappointment. Will your disappointment ruin your day, week and life or will you have a short pity party and choose to move on? That day, we decided to skip the pity party and just move on. Just a day later, we came back and had the celebration for which we had all been hoping and we got to enjoy the anticipation for another 24 hours.

I'm thankful for our friend Chad Gregory, who is the former Chairman of the Board of Directors for *Heart for Africa* U.S. that pulled out his sword and helped us navigate through the turbulent time of board division. His work resulted in a united U.S. Board with a vision for HOPE that included water. I'm also grateful for our friend Tim Lambert, who is the former Chairman of the Board of Directors for *Heart for Africa* (Canada), who also fought the water fight with us from beginning to end. He was the one who started using the phrase "water security" in conversations and Board meetings, and his belief in the importance of this goal never wavered. Thank you, Chad and Tim, from the Maxwell family and the entire *Heart for Africa* family.

Becoming water-secure would not have happened without the vision, guts, tenacity, patience, support, and financial gifts of so many individuals, organizations, and foundations. Many of you reading this chapter were present for some or all of this story. You with us, cried with us, prayed with us, and celebrated with us. Thank you to each of you! It takes a village to raise a child and it takes an even larger village to create water security for the future of that child and all who follow behind.

Being water-secure is a BIG DEAL. *Water is life.*

[1] U.S. Department of Agriculture, "2012 Census Highlights: Farm Economics," ACH12-2, May 2014. See also Environmental Working Group, Farm Subsidy Database, https://farm.ewg.org.

CHAPTER NINE

Fire

In July 2018, Ian and I were sitting on our patio, enjoying the sunset overlooking the farm, and he made a brief comment that would have a lasting impact on many people's lives. He said, "Next year is the 10th anniversary of Project Canaan. We should do something."

"That's a great idea," I thought, and then we started brainstorming and making plans for an event that I started to call epic in the early days of planning. I had no idea how "epic" that event would really be! Invitations went out, volunteers signed up to come on a special 11-day service trip, musicians were lined up, and we started planning. We didn't have a building large enough for all of the expected guests, VIPs, and our children and staff, so we had to think outside the box. Ian had the vision for an amphitheater from the early drawings of Project Canaan, but we could never quite figure out where it should go. As we worked on the plans for the big celebration, we knew that we wanted the amphitheater built for the event and that gave us a hard deadline to get it done.

We got on our ATVs and drove all over the property, looking for the right location. When we drove through the bush that ran alongside the Living Water Dam, we knew instantly that the amphitheater would go there, with a beautiful dam-made lake in the backdrop. We didn't know anyone who had ever built an amphitheater, but how hard could it be? There was Google, YouTube, and our friend Pete Wilkerson; he owns SCAPES Landscaping in Georgia and has been responsible for the land planning and the placement of roads and buildings all over Project Canaan. Collectively, we came up with a plan, a rough drawing, and then, brought in some local engineers to help with designing a stage that wouldn't end up sliding into the water in the middle of a children's performance. That would be bad.

There were so many things that needed to be done for the anniversary that the amphitheater was left to the last because the other construction, roads, maintenance, and performance items took higher priority. In early June, we had to decide if the amphitheater was a go or a no-go, and after much discussion and prayer, we decided to push the button and go for it. We hired a local Swazi builder who had no idea what an amphitheater was, but was a hard worker and took direction very well. I became the job "forewoman" and we started to build.

Gabion baskets were ordered and the children started making piles of stones to fill the baskets from around the whole farm. Everywhere we drove, we found two-foot piles of stones that we could transport to the worksite. I didn't realize that we would need many, many large truckloads of stones to fill the wire baskets, but the children loved being involved and participating in the project.

Once the gabion baskets were in place, filled, and wired shut, the 13x7-yard concrete pad was poured, then, we had a stage. Standing on the stage, looking up at the sandy hill and bush, we just didn't know if we could make it happen in time. The expression "Where there is a Willis, there is a way" was often used in my early days (my maiden name is Willis and this expression drove me forward each day). I would spend several hours making sure that the line of retaining wall block seating was even with the fishing line attached to the back of the stage. Then, the dirt would be brought in by the truckload to backfill the block wall. Center stairs were also built out of retaining block and each row got longer and longer. The men worked very hard hauling blocks, hammering in rebar, mixing, and pouring wheelbarrows full of wet concrete into the center of the blocks to add stability. Then, we hit a big rock and could not make our half-circles go any farther, so we reversed the curve and started building our "box seats" up on the top.

From the first day of construction, it took a total of 35 working days to complete the amphitheater, which seats more than 1,000 people. Only a few days later, it became the focal point of our 10th-anniversary celebration. That, in and of itself, was epic.

On July 18, 2019, we hosted a grand event to celebrate. So much had been accomplished in the first 10 years and we wanted to stop and give thanks for the Lord's provision of funds, expertise, and knowledge that had come together to make the vision a reality. We were honored to have the Deputy Prime Minister, Themba Masuku, as our VIP speaker, as well as dozens of current and past *Heart for Africa* board members, 100+ trip volunteers, almost all of our staff, and all of our children (except our babies). The event lasted three hours and our children sat perfectly for the entire gathering. They were laughing, cheering, and dancing along with the rest of our guests. I was so very proud of them all and thankful that they could be a part of a historical time marker.

The event was themed "Rooted in Love" with Ephesians 3:16-19 being our focus. It says, *"I pray that out of his glorious riches he may strengthen you with power through his Spirit in your inner being, so that Christ may dwell in your hearts through faith. And I pray that you, being rooted and established in love, may have power, together with all the Lord's holy people, to grasp how wide and long and high and deep is the love of Christ, and to know this love that surpasses knowledge—that you may be filled to the measure of all the fullness of God."*

I was the emcee for the event, introducing each speaker or performance, helping to weave together the story of HOPE that was unfolding right in front of our eyes, literally and figuratively. It was a scalding hot day, despite being in the middle of our winter, and the sun was directly in my eyes as I stood at the podium. I distinctly remember standing on the stage, looking up to my left to give my eyes a break from the sun and I saw smoke rising up over the mountain. This is not an unusual sight during the winter because fire breaks are being burned to avoid runaway fires that get out of control. Hunters burn grass to chase wild game out into the open and vandals light fires to try to scare us or others away.

Ian sent a team of guys up to check on the fire. They came back and reported that it was on the other side of the mountain in the community called Gebeni and there was no need for us to worry. The event continued and was a huge success, with children performing songs, dance, poems, and acting out a play about how Project Canaan came into existence.

The crowd laughed, cried, cheered, and celebrated 10 years of God's faithfulness, goodness, and provision. We ended the gathering by planting a tree and praying that we all might remain rooted in love. Then everyone enjoyed a piece of celebratory cake that was made by our very own kitchen staff.

After the festivities were over and everyone had gone home, we headed to the house for a shower, a cool drink on the patio, and a delicious dinner with our family. Chloe, Spencer, Spencer's girlfriend Jane, and his friend Andrew from his Master's degree program at Queen's University all came with us for the big event. We were so blessed to have them all home for the week-long celebration. Spencer and Andrew hopped on the ATVs and drove up to the top of the mountain, while Ian, Chloe, Jane, and I remained home to just relax and chat. Ian and I were the first to the patio and, as we dropped into our chairs and looked out onto the farm, we could smell smoke. Not at all concerned, but always aware of the fire, we got up and walked to the end of our patio to see a long line of fire coming down the mountain toward us. We could hear the crackling of the fire as it ate through tall grass and winter-dry brush and settled onto larger trees and branches. We could also hear the voices of Denis and his team, who were there to "switch" off the fire with switches (tree branches used to beat out the fire on the ground). There is no way to get water to these remote areas and mountains, so fire prevention is our best way to handle fire. Denis and his team cut and burn 16+ miles of firebreaks every year and 2019 was no different. He was confident that they could switch out the fires, but if not, he knew that there were firebreaks around all the buildings and fields. What he (and we) had not taken into consideration was that the wind was soon to pick up a speed that resulted in 40 hours of firefighting that would almost finish us all off.

As the sun was going down, the flames were starting to rise. As anyone knows who has been in a fire, things happen very quickly and there is little time to stop and make a plan. The fire was suddenly rushing down to the newly built "Swazi homestead," complete with a stunningly beautiful thatched grass roof. I called Allen, a senior supervisor from the children's campus, to come down with some men to help switch out the fire. Minutes later Allen was standing on the outside of our electric fence (which we hadn't had a minute to turn off) and asked for matches, so that he could run down to the Swazi homestead and light a fire around the home to burn the dry grass back to meet the fire that was rushing forward. Without electrocuting either of us, matches were passed through and the guys disappeared into the bush down the mountain. Ultimately Allen's immediate action saved those two newly built buildings from being burned to the ground.

As Allen headed down the mountain, Denis's team was growing in numbers. I still don't know how that happened, since all of his workers had already left for home. They continued to fight the fire. Suddenly, the wind whipped up and the fire was burning up the mountain toward The Lodge, a 10-room building that houses our long-term volunteers. We were on the phone with those staying there to warn them. As the fire roared up the hill, Spencer and Andrew's ATVs raced in our front gate from their mountain-top excursion, covered in what they later described as "raining ash." They had been relaxing at the top of Hope Mountain when they saw smoke over the mountaintop. As we had all been assured that the fires were on the other side of the mountain earlier in the day, they weren't worried. It wasn't until their journey back down the mountain that they saw the fires were on the mountainside by our house and they kicked it into high gear.

This was not Spencer's first fire and he knew exactly what to do. The guys put on long pants, long-sleeve shirts, jumped into knee-high snake boots, and ran back out the gate to cut tree branches and join Denis and his team. Darkness had arrived and the smoke in the air was evident by the light the fire provided to show the smoky cloud above us.

Chloe, Jane, and I stood pretty much helpless on the inside of our compound gate. We turned off the electric fencing, passed water and soft drinks through the fence to anyone who passed by, and turned on a sad little hose that didn't bear much water. Just then, one of Denis' guys ran down the side of our fence, lighting another small fire to try to burn back the grass closest to our home, so that the fire didn't jump over into our yard. Unfortunately, the man misunderstood the instruction to go down our fence and continue straight down toward the farm. Instead, he lit a fire all the way around our fence line, completely surrounding us with fire. Ian had been on the phone with various people around the farm with instructions for help and safety, but suddenly he was running up to the fence to tell the guy to stop. Well, it was too late. The wind changed again and the fire was heading down to the volunteer house beside us called the "Moringa Guest House," where six volunteers were staying at the time, including our friends Jere and Janet Scott. Chloe, Jane, and I looked up to the sky only to see the circle of smoke getting smaller and squeezing out the night. Soon we would be in a bubble of smoke and we were frozen.

As previously mentioned, the fires burned for 40 hours and I can't possibly tell you every terrifying minute of those 40 hours, but I will attempt to give you a few touchpoints that I recall from those days. After the fires passed our house, the Moringa Guest House, and down past the Harps' house, they were either put out with hoses, beaten out with switches, or lost their oxygen. Everyone, except for Denis's team, went to sleep and even the wind took its rest, but only for a few hours. In the early hours of the next morning, we were called, again. The wind was awake and blowing the fires back toward the Harp house, up past Moringa, lighting up electrical poles and anything else in its way, and was heading back up to our house, burning bush that it had missed on the way down. Spencer and Andrew were on their ATVs heading down to the farm and across to join Ian, Denis, long-term volunteers Jacob, Arlyn, and the rest of the team as the fire was heading toward a 100,000-gallon newly installed water tank. Meanwhile, the Harps, Scotts, and other long-term volunteers worked to keep their homes safe. Hours later, everyone was back in bed and we thought the fires were finished. Little did we know that they had hardly started.

Thursday morning was another beautiful winter day, the temperature around 75°F with blue sky and bright sun. The only thing that was different on that day was the lingering smell of smoke, the burnt, black mountainside, and the feeling of exhaustion. We had not even begun to talk about the celebration that was only 24 hours earlier, but instead, we woke up with our clothes, hair, and bedding smelling smoke. Ian had an all-day meeting scheduled with Tim Lambert and our agriculture team and he was looking forward to brainstorming ideas to develop a more robust strategic plan for the months and years to come.

All of the 100+ volunteers who had traveled to Eswatini for the celebration had gone on a game drive for the day with some of our older children, which left a really quiet day for Spencer, Chloe, their friends, and me. In fact, the only thing I had to do that day was to go pick up pizza at the local golf resort called Nkonyeni (pronounced "N-cone-yen-ee"). Nkonyeni is located four miles from Project Canaan and that is where our short-term volunteer teams typically stay when they visit. The accommodations are safe, comfortable, and convenient. They have air conditioning, security, Wi-Fi (sometimes), and a beautiful clubhouse with a thatched grass roof that is 65-feet high and the entire dining experience open to the African air and beautiful sunsets. I took a leisurely drive in Ian's car over to Nkonyeni to pick up pizza lunch for Ian and the team, and as I was pulling into the clubhouse, I received a call from William, our irrigation specialist from Kenya, who, who never calls me. He spoke very quickly and very calmly, but asked me to please call all the Emseni men to run toward the teacher housing as the wind had whipped up, again, and the fire had just jumped over the Harps' house and was racing toward the baby home.

Once again, Allen and the guys went to the rescue while Ian and the men with whom he had been meeting jumped into my car and drove down to the baby home. They quickly moved into action to try to keep the fire away from the baby home, but Ian got caught with his back against the outside of the electric fence, which is always off during the day, as he was trying to put out the fire before it hit the short, dry grass on the baby campus. As a flame flared up in his face, singeing his eyebrows, eyelashes, and hair, he dove to the right and landed hard on his knee and hip. Meanwhile, 40 babies under the age of 18 months were being evacuated from their home and into the toddler home.

I drove like a madwoman back to the farm and called Ian to see where he was. He said he was in the Litsemba field, but all I could see were flames, billowing smoke, and large round bales of hay on fire starting to roll down the hill. Just then, out of the smoke, walked Ian. I jumped out of his car and he jumped in, taking off down the hill; then Chloe appeared out of the smoke and told me she didn't know where Spencer was. From the other side of the road, Spencer and Andrew came out of the smoke. He said, "Mom, no one is in charge here!" I said, "You are!"

Now, in hindsight, that was an epic mom fail. Why would I automatically deputize my son to be in charge of fires that were burning wildly up and down, back and forth through our land? But Spencer took off down the hill with a team of people running behind. I know that not everyone believes in the Holy Spirit, but I do, and I believe that it was the Holy Spirit who prompted Ian a short while afterward to take a random turn onto our newly made soccer field. He couldn't see the road through the smoke as he drove down the hill and headed up the other side, but when he got to the top of the pitch, he saw a bunch of people hiding under the wooden stage that had been built for our big "Music on the Mountain" event scheduled for the last day of this historic week. The fire was heading directly toward the stage and there was no way for them to get out as the smoke engulfed the stage. Ian pulled up and, in his quiet, self-effacing style, said, "Hey, how's it going? Anyone need a ride?" With that invitation, our kids, their friends, and another five Swazis jumped into Ian's car and he drove them to safety.

For the next few hours, the fires raced up and down the mountain, getting within feet of a building; then, the wind would suddenly turn and push the fire in the opposite direction. Team leaders from the farm were in full action with dozens of Swazis working to put fires out or divert new fires, running dozens of miles that day with no time for food or rest. They simply couldn't be in all places at all times. We do have a water bowser that carries 550 gallons of water. It has a pump and hose that can be used to put out small fires and it sits on a trailer that is pulled by a tractor. On that particular day the trailer had a flat tire and no one was able to fix it in the heat of the moment, so they continued fighting fires with tree branches.

I believe that we had other protectors standing guard. It was as if angels were standing at each building and then blowing the fire away when it got too close. The fire burned around the baby campus and then jumped over to the schools, where it met up with fire that had come down that side of the mountain, only to create an inferno with flames that were easily 40 feet high. The whole mountain was on fire and all we could do was continue to evacuate people. I drove quickly down to the Khutsala Artisans and evacuated anyone who was left there and not helping fight the fires. Then, I drove down to the clinic to load my truck up with water to distribute to all those in the smoke and fire. When I got there, I could see the fire moving swiftly and eagerly to the medical clinic and when I ran inside to make sure no one was there, I was shocked to see our two dentists, Dr. Mark McGee and Dr. Stuart Coe, hard at work, with ash floating around the clinic! Of course, they had no way of knowing that Project Canaan was on fire and the fire was at their doorstep. They had their heads, hands, and minds in people's mouths. Everyone was evacuated from the building and I headed back up to Khutsala to make sure everyone got out.

I have learned that Swazis don't move quickly in an emergency. In fact, they may even slow down. It could be that I am talking so fast and giving so many instructions that they can't possibly keep up, but I was glad that I went back up and pushed the last few people out. The whole day was a game of musical cars with people jumping in and out of any moving vehicle that was going in the direction they needed to go — and we could have used so many more.

In a moment, I had Dr. McGee and Sarah Windham from our U.S. office in my truck. The fire was raging toward Khutsala and on the other side of it was the beautiful thatched roof chapel that had been built in honor of my birth father, whom I never met and is now dead. Spencer had gone down to the Farm Managers Building to try to get a hose that could start watering down the roof, on the off chance that the fire would get there; however, the hose was too small, the attachment didn't fit to the handwashing sink, and the water pressure was too low. Just then I saw an ember break away from the blaze that was easily 100 feet from Khutsala, which stood boldly between the fire and the chapel. It flew up and over Khutsala as if it had wings and its flight path planned, landing directly on the dry grass that made the thatch roof. There were people inside the chapel and all around because they were preparing to water down the roof. I started screaming like a crazy person for everyone to get away from the chapel. Sarah had the peace of mind to calmly and firmly tell everyone to remove the wooden benches, the pulpit, and the memorial plaque and put them in a delivery truck that had just pulled up to the chapel. I have no idea why it was there, other than the Lord sent it to load up His pulpit, benches, and plaque.

We all stood back and watched as the grass went up in a horrific growl of fire, flames, and smoke with a sound that I may never forget. I had been live Facebook streaming for about 30 minutes at this point because I didn't know if any of us were going to live and there was no time to call anyone to tell them what was going on. There was nothing anyone could do. I just wanted the world to see what we were seeing and living through so that they could pray with us. Dr. McGee is an incredible photographer and when that spark landed on the roof of the chapel, I leaned in the window and asked him to please take photos as the chapel burned to the ground within minutes. After the roof collapsed, the wooden poles that held the mighty weight started to burn, and then, it was just a pile of black rubble. I wept. Just then Chloe came around the corner in another vehicle, got out of her car, and wept with me. Everyone who was there just stood and stared. There was nothing anyone could do and it was already over.

Several weeks later, at a *Heart for Africa* Board meeting, one of our members, Robert Holmes, made a statement that profoundly impacted us all. He said, "Could it be that the Lord sacrificed His house so that all of the others could be saved?" It was clear to us all that the Lord had saved all but one of the buildings and we are thankful for His protection.

Throughout the day, I would check in with Ian or he would check in with me. We were in different vehicles doing different things. Ian was literally going from hot spot to hot spot (pardon the pun), checking on what was under control and what wasn't under control and needed to be under control. Ian and I have worked side by side for many years—12 years at ONYX and 15 years at Heart for Africa—and we know how each other thinks, how each other works, and what each other does well. I was mostly watching out for people (moving, evacuating, recruiting, delivering water, etc.), and Ian was doing everything else. He was driving the "mobile fire command vehicle," which was in constant contact with various people who were responsible for different areas of the farm. At times, he and his co-commander for the day, Tim, were jumping out to cut fire switches and beat the fire; then, they were scanning for new signs of smoke. They hiked up through thick African bush to find flare-ups and call in a team to put them out.

One of the most significant moments of the day was when a man from the Nkonyeni Golf Estate showed up at our front gate. Their Estate Manager, Ryan, and his team, including waiters who had served our volunteer team breakfast that morning, had come to help. They instructed us to get a group of people and drop them every 50 feet down the main road. Spencer loaded up a vehicle with Khutsala Artisans and drove down the road dropping off the guys. Next, the Nkonyeni team lit small fires along the road to start a burn toward the big fires that were now leaving the Project Canaan property and rushing over the hill. The hope was that the two would meet and the fire would be put out. If this didn't work, other neighboring farms and the golf estate itself would be at high risk. The men who were dropped on the road were there to make sure the new fire didn't jump the road, but rather burned up the hill. They stood armed with tree branches and a bottle of water and, after several hours, they succeeded. The two fires met and burned out.

Meanwhile, back on Project Canaan, the fires raged back up the mountain to The Lodge. Then, they started heading toward the children's campus in the direction of the housing where over 150 of our 3 to 8-year-olds live. I told Ian that I needed a 15-minute warning to evacuate the children and everyone was on high alert. He and the whole team were watching the fire closely as it approached yet another firebreak that was meant to protect the children's homes from fire. Again, the fire crouched down low and leaped up and over the men; and the fire break, now on a race to get to the children before they could escape. Earlier I had called

Bryan Throgmorton (our long-term volunteer Program Director) and a few of my supervisors to have them prepared in case an evacuation was necessary.

Only an hour later I made the call to evacuate immediately and instructed them to very quickly get the small children in vehicles and bigger children to race down to the dairy. I asked them not to make the children fear, but they must move swiftly. I drove directly down to the Emseni Campus, the older kid's homes, and saw them all running down the hill toward the farm, through the white and black smoke, over the dam, and on to the dairy. Bryan personally went inside each house to make sure that everyone was gone and no child was left behind. He later reported there was smoke blowing through the houses and all the fire alarms in every room on every floor were going off as if they were in a bad symphony of untuned instruments. The infants had all been moved back to the El Roi baby home after the fire went past in the morning, but now unburned grass that was spared earlier in the day was burning straight toward the baby home, again. Once more we evacuated the 40 infants to the toddler home, turned all of the vehicles around, and left keys inside for an evacuation that we hoped would never come.

Where do you take 90+ infants and toddlers during an angry wildfire that seems intent on killing and destroying everything in its path? We decided that the schools would be our only chance, as the mountain upon which they are located had burned already and burned badly. We sent a runner to unlock all the doors so that they were ready for their young visitors. Diapers, wipes, clothes, blankets, bottles, and formula were at the ready.

There was never any response to any call we made to the fire department that day and the police came out to assure us that the fire department was on their way, but they were not. After a less than a courteous conversation with the police and the media that suddenly showed up at our gate to assess the situation, Ian and I reconnected at the dairy to see the big kids and reassure them that all was going to be okay. When we got there, I turned and looked back up the mountain for the first time, only to see smoke and fire engulfing the whole mountain. We couldn't see our house, the children's homes, the schools, anything. We went over to see the children and to thank them for being so obedient.

Several things were said to me that I will also never forget.

Ruth looked at me and said, "Make (mom) Janine, who will protect us?"

I responded, "Babe (dad) and I will protect you, but really it is Jesus who protects us all." She accepted that answer and walked away.

Then Ben came up to me and said, "Make (mom), we were supposed to have ice cream at 4 o'clock. Are we still going to have it?"

A reasonable question. Rome is burning, the sky is falling, our homes may be gone, but are we on track for ice cream?

I replied, "Well, Ben, not likely."

He shrugged his shoulders and said, "Okay, maybe tomorrow." And walked away.

These kids were not afraid. Yes, there was uncertainty and concern, but our staff acted so calmly and intentionally that the children felt safe and secure. If Make and Babe and all the Aunts and Uncles weren't afraid, then, they weren't going to be afraid, either. It was just another day in the life of people living on Project Canaan, a place of hope and safety.

I would be remiss not to mention one other comment that was made to us at the dairy and it was the first question asked—but I need to give you a little background first. The volunteer team that comes in July always helps us with "Camp Canaan," which is like a very customized Vacation Bible School for our children. On that particular July, we were thrilled to have our very own petting zoo for the children to learn more about animals up close. Earlier in the week, Bryan had arranged a Camp Canaan petting zoo that was located on the grass between the baby home and the toddler home. The children loved holding the one-day-old chicks, looking up close at monkeys, and petting baby farm animals. It was a magical couple of days and I honestly thought that it would be the highlight of everyone's week. So, when we first arrived at the dairy the day of the fire to see the kids, one of the children ran up, and the first thing asked was if the baby chicks were okay. I asked where they were staying; I thought all animals had been returned safely to their homes when the petting zoo closed. The children told me they were in the boy's house at Emseni 4. I wasn't going to lie, because I didn't know if Emseni 4 was still standing, but I told them that I hoped they would be fine and that I would find out. I was moved by their concern for God's creatures. The chicks were, in fact, okay.

I mentioned that we had 100+ volunteers from around the world visiting us that week and you might be wondering where they were through all this? Thankfully, they were all off of Project Canaan and were spending the day out at our church partners, feeding children, doing well-child checks, and celebrating 10 years of provision of food and hope for their communities. It was a blessing to us that they were able to be a blessing to our partners and were not in harm's way during the fires. In fact, for many, they didn't hear about the fires until the end of the day when they loaded up in their vans and headed back to the hotel for dinner.

Former Board Chairperson Susan Page said, "Our team was in a church that was really far away from Project Canaan. We first heard about the fire from our driver as we drove back to Nkonyeni. The driver was shrieking words like, "Oh, no! What? Really?" as she got info from her fellow worker at Project Canaan. And it was shocking driving down the mountain, seeing the fires all around us, not knowing that many people in the country had lost everything and several had died."

We only heard stories like Susan's and others many months later.

Just before dark, we were able to transfer the children by truck back to the Emseni Campus from the dairy, as those fires had extinguished. The babies moved back to the El Roi baby home from the toddler home, and we crawled up the hill to our house. Denis and his team were still fighting the fires as they turned toward the farm, but we just didn't have any energy left. Some of us hadn't had a bite to eat the whole day, thinking we'd have pizza for lunch. I got into the bathroom, sat on the floor, toppled over onto the pile of dirty, smoky clothes from the day before, and tears started to leak out of my eyes. Then, Ian came in and sat quietly in the dirty clothes pile beside me. Next, Chloe came and sat down in the door frame, and Spencer appeared beside Chloe.

We were dirty, covered in smoke, and had inhaled more smoke and soot than humanly safe. We were exhausted. We laughed, we cried, and then we got up and everyone went to their rooms and had a shower. Once done, Ian made the best margarita I'd ever had. We sat on our bed and looked out into the pitch-black night, watching the orange and red fires continuing to burn toward the farm. We couldn't move. We had nothing left. The fire would hopefully burn out when it reached the fields; we hoped it wouldn't burn all of the irrigation drip tape and piping. Ian's phone rang. It was Tim, who had been with us throughout the whole day, but was still in the battle. He wanted to know if we were going down to fight the fires on the farm, but Ian just said, "Nope. We can't. Our family is done."

Spencer and Drew needed to run down with one last thing: gasoline for the pump on the water bowser, which finally had been put on a trailer with repaired tires. They dropped it off, came back home, and had a hot shower. Denis, Tim, and the team were clever and turned on the irrigation pipes, which kept them from burning and redirected the fire away from the pipes.

Forty hours after the fire began, it was out, only 40 feet away from the greenhouse and 20 feet from the 5,000 laying hens. While there was extensive damage to the farm and fences, the only one of 65 buildings that had burned was the chapel.

No one present during the 2019 fires will forget the depth and breadth of the destruction that took place, and no one will ever forget the protection and peace that came with the devastation.

God was with us through it all. He never left us, nor forsook us. Within weeks of the fires being extinguished, there was a lady in Texas who read my blog as I shared about our desire to rebuild the chapel and double it in size. The cost to do so was approximately $40,000. Her heart was moved and she took action by writing a check for the full amount and putting it in the mail that very day. We started rebuilding the chapel the following week and the new chapel was rebuilt within months. *Amazing!*

One year later, on July 19, 2020, we gathered again to give thanks for all that the Lord had done. The children performed, the Swazis sang, and Ian dedicated the newly rebuilt chapel to the Lord. Joshua, the first child to arrive on Project Canaan, cut the ribbon. After that, we moved all the children out of the chapel for a surprise. Ian had misters (like sprinklers) installed in the grass roof so that if (and when) there is another fire, we can just flick the lever and turn on the water to soak the grass roof. The children squealed with delight and started dancing and running into the water. You can't turn on a sprinkler with children around and not expect them to get wet! I quickly jumped on Facebook Live so that friends around the world could join in our celebration. The water kept pouring, the puddles started to build up, and more and more children joined in to get wet! It was such a fun way to end the day of celebration and very different from the year before.

It was later that evening while sitting on the patio, reflecting upon all that God had accomplished in the past year, when I started reading the comments on my Facebook post. One person commented that the water pouring down off the roof looked like the chapel itself was being baptized. My friend David Bryant wrote, "The children marching around the chapel reminds me of Joshua marching around the walls of Jericho. The Lord destroyed the plans of the enemy and caused the walls of our fears to crumble and painful memories of last year's fires to be transformed into victory."

Jesus didn't sacrifice His own house to save all the others, but allowing it to burn and then seeing it rebuilt for His glory were profound moments in my life. Thank you, Jesus, for your love and protection.

CHAPTER TEN

Angels Among Us

When Ian was a little boy, he was lying in bed one morning and woke up to hear who he thought was his parents sitting on the side of his bed, talking about him. Of course, he wanted to hear what they were saying, so he lay very quietly with both eyes shut tight. He couldn't hear everything they were saying and it didn't sound like his parent's voices, but they were whispering so he strained to hear them speak. He heard one of them say to the other, "This one is going to be a handful. We are going to have to keep a close eye on him."

What? Were they really talking about him? He opened his eyes and started to sit up to ask what they meant by that? There was light coming in through the basement window so the room was not completely dark. When he sat up, the two were gone. He ran to the door, which was closed, and he assumed that they had (very) quickly run out into the hall, but they were nowhere to be found. Ian ran up the stairs and through the house to his parent's bedroom, only to find them both sound asleep in bed.

He knew at that moment that he had been visited by two angels. There was no other explanation. He had heard the voices, felt them sitting on the bed, and felt them stand up. They were real and he knew it. This is not a story that Ian has told many people, as not everyone believes in angels, but I want to share several angel stories with you to believe or not.

When Spencer was a newborn baby, we were taking him to Ottawa to meet the family for the first time. It was a five-hour drive, a lovely one on a warm July day. We stopped at a rest stop along the highway and I moved past a very long line coming out of the women's bathroom, so that I could get to the baby changing table and change Spencer's diaper. There had to have been more than 25 women in line to use the facilities. As I was just starting to undress my new baby, a woman swept up across from me, put her hand on my precious child, and asked if she could pray for him.

I was so taken aback by a total stranger touching my child that I just said yes. The woman prayed very specifically for protection over Spencer's life and that he would come to know the Lord at a very young age and then she walked away toward the toilet stalls. I was shocked and quickly changed Spencer's diaper and rushed out to find Ian waiting for us; I reported what had just happened. Because I wanted to ask the woman who she was and what had prompted her to do such an unusual thing in a public washroom, we stood right outside the door and waited for her to come out.

The line dwindled until there was no line left, so I handed Spencer to Ian and went in search of the lady, but she was nowhere to be found. There was no other exit from that washroom, every stall was empty, and she did not walk out through the door where I'd been standing. I looked at Ian and we both asked at the same time, "Do you think she was an angel?"

I believe in angels and I believe that they are here on earth. I also believe in guardian angels who are sent by the Lord to protect us. I don't know if everyone has one, but I have always felt that there was someone standing nearby to protect me. I specifically remember feeling a heavenly protection in the slums of Kenya, in a village in Malawi, and in some skanky bars in Alphabet City, New York (back in the old days, of course). I don't know if my theology on this is correct or if people would dispute what we have experienced, but I have also seen them at at work in Eswatini since starting to work here.

I remember getting a call from a Social Welfare officer who said that a baby had been found in a pit latrine and was at the hospital. When I arrived to pick up the baby and bring her home, the social worker stopped me and told me a bit more about the story. She was doing her investigation and had actually found the young mother who'd dumped the baby. The girl was shocked that the baby was found and was alive because she had given birth five days earlier. (This is the baby I mentioned in Chapter 3!) She had wrapped the newborn in a baby blanket before dropping her into the pit of human waste, which obviously saved the newborn from being burned by the acid waste. It probably protected her from what was released from each person who had made their way to that toilet in the five days she'd spent at the bottom. However, a baby blanket couldn't have saved her from the gasses being emitted from the waste or the lack of water that would cause dehydration or the lack of food, which would cause developmental delay and death.

How *did* she live for those five days?

I was immediately given a beautiful vision. I saw a guardian angel sitting in the human waste, holding the baby in his or her arms, protecting her from any harm, and singing sweet songs of praise to her heavenly Father over the baby, while the baby slept quietly and peacefully—for five long days. Finally, it was time for her to go and the angel released her to cry out when someone was using the toilet, again; the family and the police were called, and this little one was taken to the hospital.

I have no proof that this is what actually happened, but that is what I have in my head every single time I see that child running up to give me a hug.

In another instance, I was driving past the Mawelawela Women's prison and saw a newspaper headline that said, "Inmate gives birth—attempts to kill the baby." *What the what?* I immediately picked up my phone and called the social worker at the prison to ask if there was anything I could do to help. She said, "Yes! Please come get this baby!" So I u-turned and drove through the prison gates. I went through the usual routine of handing in my ID, taking off my jewelry, watch, leaving my phone, etc., and went up to the Commandant's office, which is where I first met baby Mbali. Sitting on the floor was a woman who had given birth the day before. Allegedly the prison was unaware that she had arrived pregnant and she'd hid it from everyone. (She was very small and thin.) She had been in labor throughout the night and delivered the baby while everyone else had gone for breakfast. She'd then strangled the newborn baby with her own hands, leaving fingernail marks on the baby's neck.

Once the baby stopped breathing, she had placed her in the garbage can in the washroom and put garbage on top of the dead baby.

Then, she made her way to breakfast, but as the placenta had not been delivered, she was bleeding profusely and another inmate reported her to a guard. The guard immediately accused her of trying to abort a baby, which is a crime here, but the young woman cried out and assured them that she had not aborted a baby. They continued to scold her until she took them to the garbage can and showed them the dead baby.

The prison nurse was called and immediately started giving the baby CPR, even though the infant had been dead for some time. Suddenly the baby gasped for air and came back to life! The nurse told me that her grayish skin started to turn pink and the baby opened her eyes. She was alive!

As this story was recited to me, I was holding the newborn baby in my arms and weeping, both at the tragedy of the situation, but also at the miracle. How did this baby come back to life? Was there a guardian angel standing guard over the garbage can? That infant came home with us that very day and the mother remained in prison.

Mbali is now a 6-year-old girl who is healthy, smart, and has no lingering problems from oxygen loss. The fingernail marks are still visible on her neck, but only to someone who knows that they are there. Every time I see her I give thanks for her life.

Recently, we have been speaking with the older children about making choices and helping them understand the differences between a good choice and a bad choice, as well as what the repercussions are of each.

Ian has often shared the story of the headmaster of the high school we attended together telling students that when you wake up in the morning, you have a choice to make – as to whether you want to be in a good mood or a bad mood; if you don't make that choice, you leave the door wide open for circumstances or people to influence your mood for the day. It was an important life lesson for him and one that has helped direct his cheerful disposition every morning.

I know a little girl who wakes up every morning and chooses joy as her default mood, though she has a lot of valid reasons not to make that choice. This little girl's name is Joy.

Joy was burned badly when she was only a few days old. She was allegedly burned in what is commonly known here as "Lubane."

The Swazi Observer of June 2018 says, "According to the Traditional Healers Association in Swaziland, Lubane is when fire erupts out of nowhere and is associated with the use of black magic. The intention of Lubane is to hurt the person experiencing it and often leads to death if untreated. A person goes and raises a dead person with fire and uses them as an invincible arsonist who, after touching anything, will leave it on fire."

No one seems to know the origin of the mysterious fire, but Joy received third-degree burns on her face, leaving her without a nose, lips, an ear, with one eye melted and closed, and with no hair on most of her head. Joy is also missing a piece of her skull that should be protecting the main artery in her head. (You can see her heartbeat through the skin on her skull.) There was no burn care available to her in Swaziland and she suffered at home in a very poor rural homestead — the so-called "deep Swaziland."

Joy's father was put in prison and her mother had to go far away to find work to support the family, so Joy was raised by her gogo and khokho (grandmother and great grandmother). Every day, Joy would get out of bed and choose joy while she went to fetch firewood, cook pap over the fire, or even fetch water from the river where children are rumored to disappear. Joy never walked; she only skipped. When she met someone on the road she would try to smile, but without lips, the person she greeted could not see her smiling from her mouth; they could, though, see a happy, bubbly little girl and a smile with her one eye.

When it was time to go to school, Joy was so excited because she would meet new friends. Her gogo and khokho were very worried about how the children would accept Joy and whether they would be afraid of her or hurt her, but they also knew Joy's ability to make everyone happy and love her. The time arrived for Joy to go to first grade and off she went with her older brothers and sisters, but the children at the school were very cruel to this seriously disfigured young girl. Even when they called her an animal and spewed other words of hate at her, she always stayed joyful, trying to show the other students that she was just a fun, normal girl—but, really, there is nothing normal about Joy.

One day, a group of children surrounded her and started to attack her. Her sister tried to step in and protect Joy, as she always did, but the day ended with her index finger broken and her elbow shattered. Joy never returned to school because her gogo knew that it just wasn't safe for her and the teachers were not interested in protecting her from the bullies.

I learned about Joy through a social worker who called me in tears. She had been at the men's prison and a prisoner had begged her to go and check on his 8-year-old daughter; he said she had a few burns on her face and she needed to be checked on. The social worker was able to do a home visit a few weeks later and called me, begging for help. She told me she would send photos through WhatsApp and warned me not to look at them until the morning when I was fresh and rested. I actually did as she suggested because I get some horrific photos from social workers via WhatsApp, without warning, and I am not always emotionally prepared to see what they have sent. When I opened the photos the next day, I was aghast. How could this truly have happened and how could she not have received any help in eight years?

Ian and I are met daily with challenges about which we can do nothing. There are so many people in need, so much disease, so many hungry children, so much pain and suffering, and we simply can't help everyone. However, seeing a child in such pain is not something with which I can live if there is a way to get her help.

There were many challenges. First, we don't accept children over the age of 24 months and Joy was older than our eldest children, so that was certainly an exception that we could not make. Second, she would need years of very costly facial reconstructive surgery in addition to counseling, special education, and more. We prayed and asked the Lord for direction and I immediately felt I should reach out to our friends at Global Medical Relief Fund, who were so helpful with baby Barbara. They replied and said that they would absolutely help her and that the very best facial plastic surgeons are at the Shriners Hospital in Boston. "All" we had to do was find a host family in Boston to care for Joy and a volunteer guardian to travel with her and care for her as there was no family member who was able to do that.

Sheesh, this was a tough one.

I only know one family in Boston, so I sent them a cryptic email and asked for a FaceTime call. I wish I could tell you all the details of this incredible story, but I can't at this time. Suffice it to say that Eileen and Joe Habelow said "yes" to long-term medical house guests and their lives were changed forever by a little girl who chooses "joy" each and every day.

The next step was to figure out who was going to travel with her, how to get a passport, U.S. visa, and how to prepare this young girl physically, emotionally, and psychologically for travel to the U.S. for an extended stay with strangers during extreme surgeries. I sat down with our Children's Campus supervisors and nurses to talk through a plan that we thought could work.

Then, I approached a smart, young Swazi lady named Nokwanda, who had just graduated from university and was working in our front office. I explained the assignment and asked her if she would pray about being the guardian. Nokwanda had never been to the U.S. before, had never flown, and there were lots of "firsts" that she and Joy would be experiencing, but without hesitation, she agreed. The plan was coming together.

After further prayer and hours of discussion, our team decided that we should bring Joy to Project Canaan to acclimate her to "western living" before she went to Boston for three months of surgeries. She would need to learn to use a toilet that flushes (not an outhouse or forest), sleep in a bed (rather than on a mat on the mud floor with her grandmother, great grandmother, brother, and sister), turn lights on and off (their home has no electricity), and live with other people who are not her own family. We also wanted her to gain some weight so that she would be prepared for extensive surgeries in the months ahead. Her grandmother told us that she always complained that she was hungry, and there was very little food at the homestead. She didn't speak any English, so we wanted to work on that, too. We also felt concerned over how we could bring this disfigured child to our home when we have so many young children who might be frightened.

So we made another plan: We started telling the children about a girl who was badly burned and we started praying with the kids for her every night. A week after that, we showed them photos of Joy, put the photo up in the living room of the bigger kids, and prayed again. I was told during the week that several of the children asked if Joy could come and live with them.

The following week it was time to bring Joy to her new temporary residence. It was heartwarming to see how much our kids cared. They even asked, "Why can't Make Janine help Joy?" After a three-hour drive, we met Joy and her gogo on the side of the road because there was no way to actually get to the house where they lived by car during the rainy season. Her gogo and Joy had left their stick-and-mud house at 5:30 a.m. and walked for two hours to meet us. We found them in the shade under a tree, trying to stay cool on a day that was 104°F(40°C).

Her gogo shook Joy's hand to say goodbye; there were no hugs, no tears—just goodbye and then Joy got into the car with total strangers, knowing she wouldn't return home for months. When we got to Emseni 3 where the big girls live, we had six girls come in at a time to meet her. We also had chocolate for Joy to give each child as a "hello" gift. The girls were wonderful, all except for a few who were a bit hesitant. It was a very hot day, so we turned on the sprinklers and gave Joy her first-ever bathing suit. Within minutes, the girls were all running in and out of the sprinkler, with Joy as the leader of the pack. By nightfall, everyone was okay with their new friend. When an Auntie asked Joy if she was sad or scared, she replied, "No, I'm okay; I have lots of new girlfriends now." She chose joy in a situation that could otherwise have been terrifying.

Joy and Nokwanda were on a journey together for the past two years while living in Boston, going through her many surgeries, being stuck in the U.S. during the Covid-19 pandemic, moving to Georgia to attend school between surgeries, and living with different host families every month. (The Habelow family moved to Florida, so the girls could no longer stay in Boston.) Eventually, they were able to get a repatriation flight back to Eswatini and arrived home eight months after their intended return.

Joy brought joy to each person she met in every city she visited. We have seen her skip inside the hospital to have cranioplasty and sing *Frozen* songs while her new lips were draining out through a stent. She says "thank you" after every meal and offers to do the dishes. I don't know what plans the Lord has for this child, but I sure am glad that we were invited to be a part of her life story.

Joy has been accepted here as a special "boarding school student" and lives with the older girls when she is in Eswatini between surgeries; she continues to bring joy to our home and school. From the first day Joy arrived at Project Canaan, I have often wondered if she really is an angel among us because she sure doesn't seem to have the flaws of being human.

Hebrews 13:2 reminds us to, *"Stay on good terms with each other, held together by love. Be ready with a meal or a bed when it's needed. Why, some have extended hospitality to angels without ever knowing it!"* When I read that scripture, I often stop, look around and wonder who around me could be an angel. Have you ever done that? It can be a sobering experience because it may not be the angelic-looking little girl or boy smiling up at you or even the elderly person who is so gently giving you counsel and holding your hand. It just might be the person at whom you are peering through the prison bars or the person who just fell out of the front door of the local bar.

One day, a baby arrived at our gate and he was obviously very sick. In fact, the social worker brought him to us because the hospital couldn't and wouldn't help. There was mass confusion around the case, resulting in the child falling through the cracks of the "healthcare system." The baby had suffered for the whole 15 months of his life and had been in and out of the hospital many times as he was starving to death at home.

Baby Elvis (as we called him) was the ninth-born child to a woman who was eight months pregnant when he arrived. She had been living with her husband until he decided to leave her, and, as a result, his family kicked her and her eight children out of the homestead. She was hopeless. When the baby could no longer hold up his head and was even too weak to open his eyes, she carried him twelve miles and a half to find help at the Social Welfare office. It was when we received the phone call for help and it was an emergency arrival.

When Elvis showed up, he had all signs of severe malnutrition, called Kwashiorkor. His body was very fat and puffy, but that is because his body was storing fluid, putting pressure on his organs—particularly on his liver and heart. His feet and hands were hot to the touch, but he didn't have a fever. Nurse Anthony did a full assessment to find many problems, including his skin had split and was peeling due to the swelling from the edema, his teeth were rotten and malformed, he had severe diaper rash, severe thrush, and his whole body hurt when touched.

We followed all of our protocols and sought counsel from two doctors (our pediatrician and our HIV, TB, and malnutrition expert). We decided to keep him with us for the night and then take him to the hospital in the morning. At least, he would have the best one-on-one care for the night, along with as much of our love as was humanly possible.

We made our own special formula designed for severely malnourished children (called F75) and slowly started his treatment. There was no urine or stool for many hours and then he started vomiting. By the early morning hours, his breathing had become shallow, so we rushed him to the government hospital, with me driving like a crazy person and Anthony holding the baby in the back seat, fearing we would lose him during the drive.

There was a team of emergency room doctors from the U.S. in the country working on emergency medicine training, who "just happened" to come and visit us the morning before Elvis arrived. It's another long story, but the short version is that I called and told them about our emergency and that we were losing a baby. They jumped in their car at their hotel, drove 35 minutes to the hospital, ran straight into the ER, and started working. I was shocked that the doctors and nurses who were in that department just stepped back and let these foreigners (who really seemed to know what they were doing) take over. They quickly stuck an intraosseous needle deep into Elvis' thigh bone (something the Swazi nurses there had never seen before) and things started to look better quickly. An hour later, though, he took another turn for the worse.

We had been in the Emergency Department in the government hospital for four hours. It was clear that Elvis needed to be put on a ventilator and needed other life-saving equipment and supplies that were not available at a government hospital. I called a private hospital and asked if we could transfer this tiny, dying patient to them and the doctor agreed to have the Intensive Care Unit ready when we arrived.

We had to move quickly and knew that we would not be able to get the baby discharged officially before losing him. We quietly made a plan, explained it to Anthony (who would be the one having to speak in siSwati if we got into trouble), and then, I went out to my truck. I quickly drove around to the ambulance entrance and made the phone call to Anthony to tell the team to *run*! No lie, these American doctors and nurses unplugged everything to which Elvis was attached (except the Ambu bag that was pumping oxygen into his little lungs), grabbed the baby, who was now blue in the face, ran, and jumped into the back seat of my truck. The nurses tried to stop them and shouted at them for stealing, while Anthony assured them that we promised to return anything that was being "borrowed." I had a doctor with an Ambu bag manually respirating the baby and a nurse providing other care as we raced through downtown Manzini to a private hospital, all while praying for the miracle of life to continue.

We got to the hospital where the ICU team was waiting, as promised, and they raced the baby into the Intensive Care Unit. *Four* U.S. doctors and nurses and *four* Swazi doctors and nurses worked to save his life. It took 50 minutes to intubate him; the machine was breathing for him, so they could start working on the other issues.

Exhausted, we headed home and prayed that Elvis would have the strength to make it through the night and fight for another day. We gave thanks for God's perfect timing in having those ER doctors and nurses at the right place and at the right time.

At 10:10 p.m. I got the call that Elvis was dead.

I wept for Elvis; we all wept for him. While this little baby was only in our care for 30 hours, he was *our* baby. We lost our baby and hadn't even had time to get to know him or for him to know us. I do know that he was loved deeply for his last 30 hours of life and that there are a handful of people who had a life-changing experience during those 30 hours we will never forget. Did we extend hospitality to an angel without knowing it? We will never know. Was Elvis brought to us for some other reason?

Two weeks later, his 40-year-old (or older) mother gave birth to her ninth child and she had already asked that the child be given to us when he was born. She knew that she had no way to care for him and was desperate to have this baby live. Imagine giving your newborn baby to the very people with whom your lastborn child had died. Because it was a very high-risk pregnancy and she lived deep in the bush, without a real shelter or any way to quickly get to a medical facility if she went into labor, we made arrangements in advance for her to be admitted to another government hospital. We have a really good relationship with the maternity ward doctors, nurses, and social workers there and have saved many lives together as a team. They agreed to let her rest, heal from the loss of her child, and prepare for the birth of her next baby. She went into labor naturally, but then things turned bad and an emergency Cesarean section was performed. Everyone involved saw the hand of God in this situation because if she had given birth at home, deep in the bush, both mother and baby would surely have died.

While little Elvis is safe in the arms of Jesus, his little brother arrived home to Project Canaan only a few hours after being born and is now a happy and healthy little boy.

I could write a hundred more stories about angels in our presence, or miracles that I have witnessed, or stories that might help an unbeliever believe, but I would remiss if I didn't also mention the dark side of serving in a developing nation. As I said in Chapter Four, everything is hard here; however, the hardest part isn't what you might think. It's not death or disease, ignorance nor illiteracy, and it's not even frustration or failure.

It's betrayal, and sadly, it's something that we have had to get used to. We learned early on to be careful with our valuables while traveling in and through developing countries and that made logical sense. Nice cameras, phones, or even razors and lotions can be a temptation to someone living on one dollar a day. We have had things stolen out of our suitcases, backpacks, hotel rooms, and cars and we even had a terrible break-in at our home in Eswatini a few years ago. Our MacBooks and iPads were taken along with an old pink backpack and some candy from the pantry, but the burglars left a lot of damage behind while they looked for cash. That break-in happened while we were at Children's Church on Project Canaan, so it was clearly an inside job since only our immediate staff knew where we were and when we would get home. Two of our volunteers saw one of our most trusted employees drive up the hill toward our house during the service. They thought it was odd and mentioned it to me immediately following the break-in. Yet how could we begin to believe that person was involved? Could it be possible?

Over the years, we have caught people stealing generators (we followed the drag marks through the grass), found Project Canaan televisions in community homes, and even caught people stealing dairy meals to sell or perhaps fatten up their own cows. What has been most disheartening has been catching the people who are closest to us, the ones who are making the highest salaries, stealing from this ministry. I remember learning about a supervisor who was "ghosting" at least 14 employees and pocketing their salaries every month for more than a year. He was forging those workers' names every day, six days a week, and then signing for their pay (it was cash back then) and putting it in his pocket. We found over 5,000 counts of fraud before we just stopped looking further. We were devastated, brokenhearted, and could not believe that this person whom we trusted completely would betray us so badly. Ian handles these situations better than I do and he would quickly remind me that the person didn't steal from us—he stole from Jesus and Jesus saw him do it, every day, every month, for many months. Ian's wisdom and approach to God's ministry have always been a source of encouragement and calm to me. That is why I say that Ian is my rudder.

There was also the supervisor who would sell or give away leftover construction supplies at the end of a job to put money in his own pocket and gain favor with another supervisor. Then, there was the senior employee who was stealing food and supplies from our children's campus kitchen, in cahoots with another senior employee.

We can't forget the construction supervisor in business with a man from a local retailer; entire pallets of cement were offloaded in town after he'd signed the paper that said we had received it all on Project Canaan. Even as I was writing this chapter, we learned of another trusted senior employee who committed fraud by asking one of our suppliers to falsely increase an invoice so that he could pocket the extra money. He will lose his job, his livelihood, and face criminal charges that may lead to prison time after working with us for seven years.

It didn't seem to matter how many checks and balances we put in place because it was the most trusted people who were stealing. Checks and balances are important, and the more the better when serving in a developing nation, but at some point, you have to be able to trust people. That is where discipleship really gets hard.

I remember hearing stories of other children's homes having to physically hand search each employee when they left at night because so much food was stolen from the pantry. One lady was caught with a huge stick of salami under her skirt, which was a dead giveaway that something wasn't right, but she explained that her children were starving and so she felt justified taking the food from the orphanage to her home.

After hearing many stories like this, we knew that we had to do two things: first, make sure our workers have enough access to food to feed their families, so they don't have to turn into thieves to feed their children; second, have security check all bags and bodies when departing the property. We were prepared, we were counseled, and we have done both with relative success, but we still have to put our trust in people and some people will always let us down.

Sadly, this has had a significant impact on Spencer and Chloe, as they have experienced the heartbreak of betrayal. In fact, it has changed how Spencer interacts with people. I give my trust freely and if someone betrays me, they lose my trust and break the relationship; it is really hard to earn my trust back. Spencer is now the opposite. In an attempt to not be hurt by betrayal, he does not give his trust freely; it must be earned first, and then given.

Let me say loud and clear that we have many staff members we trust and we are so incredibly proud of our leadership team and department heads, but we also see that it is our children who *must* change the face of this nation. We teach them to tell the truth always. We try to instill that lying breaks relationships and healthy relationships are critical to success in life.

While I know that there are angels around and among us, not everyone sees them the way we do. If they did, they wouldn't behave the way they do. God will not be mocked.

CHAPTER ELEVEN
Building a Bridge for the Future

As we were preparing for our 10th Anniversary celebrations, Ian and I had a big *"aha"* moment. We were working on a timeline of our first 10 years and then looking forward to the next 10, and what we noticed was very interesting. In the first decade, we were able to put in all the infrastructure needed for Project Canaan, including roads, electricity, water security, food production, trades, clinic, administrative office, security, and income-generating projects. In addition to that, we have processes and procedures for all departments and a system for child intake, development, and growth. The school vision has been cast and the first four grades are built. "All" we have left to do is to continue building one Emseni dormitory each year and one classroom. When the building projects are complete, we will have 13 Emseni dormitories, a middle school, and a high school. It just so happens that our first 12th-grade class will graduate from the Project Canaan Academy in 2029, which is exactly 20 years from when we purchased the land.

That also means that, as of the time of this writing in 2020, we are 11 years into the project and "only" have nine more years to go for it to be complete. When I say "complete," I mean that the full cycle of a child arriving in the baby home to exiting high school will have been completed. That is really cool! God willing, I will be 65 years old and Ian will be 63. That seems like a reasonable age for us to step aside and let new leadership take the reins. That also gives us nine more years to continue teaching, training, and leading our team to take on the project when it is time for us to step down.

Our plan is to remain here on Project Canaan, enjoy the children, continue to provide guidance when necessary, and cheer on the team from our mountaintop deck chairs, basking in the beautiful sunrises and sunsets over the horizon.

Succession planning is a topic that has come up many times over the years. In the early days of Project Canaan, there weren't many conversations about it, but as children started to arrive, our board of directors asked frequently what would happen if we were to leave. (They meant to die.) Who would take over the ministry? What would happen to the children and the vision? We simply didn't have an answer. First, who would want to step into these crazy shoes we are wearing? Second, we were just starting to develop the infrastructure and construct buildings, so how could anyone plan to take that over? We considered those reasonable answers, but their fear and concerns were valid. What if Ian and I were in a plane crash together? Who would step in?

Here is what we did—and I strongly recommend anyone in ministry do the same. We developed an "In Case of the Death of Ian and Janine" plan. It was very detailed, starting with who to call, including contact information for key friends and family members who would need to be notified first. Then, we created a seven-day plan that included notification to government officials, partners, suppliers, and other important people who would need to know of our passing. We even included some basic funeral requests, including instruction to be buried in the Project Canaan cemetery. This would avoid any confusion or conflicts between family, board members, and employees. Our wishes are clear.

Next, we wrote a a three to six-month plan and a six to nine-month plan of what we felt needed to be done during those time periods and what wasn't urgent. There were recommendations on how to divide up our responsibilities, where new hires would need to be made, and where new oversight would need to be implemented. (Writing this chapter reminded me that the document needed updating, so I paused writing to do just that.)

It is a living, breathing document that gives everyone some peace of mind without knowing the actual "who" will take over the ministry when we are gone. We are always intentionally looking for people with natural leadership abilities, people who want to learn, grow, and be stretched. We have ongoing formal leadership training, but the very best way for us to lead is by discipling the people around us on a daily basis—walking the walk, talking the talk. Do I think it will be hard to let go when the time comes? Probably, but it has to happen. Too often the founders of an organization continue leading the organization when they are past their prime, causing all sorts of problems. The key is for the founders to be able to share the vision well enough that everyone understands it and wants to be a part of that vision. The reality is that organizations do change when leadership changes and that is okay, so long as the vision is kept at the forefront.

Who do we really think will "take over" Project Canaan when our time is finished? We believe that we are currently training the next leadership team and they, in turn, will be preparing our Project Canaan children to be the keepers and stewards of the vision since they have raised in it from the beginning.

They won't be ready to lead in a significant way in 2029 when they graduate from high school; they'll need help to cross the bridge from being a teen to adulthood. Spencer and Chloe went through a tremendous upheaval during their teen years and we kind of threw them into the deep end of life. We moved to Africa when Spencer graduated from high school and then flew back to the U.S. to get him settled in university, but he was pretty much on his own after that. He had to adult-up very quickly, with a family support system a million miles away (and very bad and slow Internet). Chloe moved to Eswatini with us and attended a local private school here, but it just wasn't a good experience. She arrived mid-year to a class that was well bonded. We made the hour drive every morning to drop her off at her school bus, upon which she spent an additional 45 minutes to get to school. At the end of the day, we reversed the travel. It was physically exhausting, emotionally draining, and left no personal time for her fun or friends.

At the end of that school year, we decided to make a change and not one that I would have ever anticipated. I have spent several weeks each year in Taiwan speaking at schools and promoting my books, which have been translated into Mandarin. Through these visits, I was introduced to an international private Christian school—Morrison Academy in Taichung, Taiwan—that primarily caters to missionary kids in Asia. I would rave about this school each time I returned home; one day Chloe asked if she could attend Morrison Academy in the next school year, to which I immediately said, "No!" She gave us all the reasons she thought going to school in Taiwan (a 12-hour flight in the opposite direction of where Spencer lived in the U.S.) made sense. Ian and I both said no, again. Then she asked if we would at least pray about it. *Sheesh!* Why don't you just throw the whole "prayer thing" in my face?

Well, it worked. We prayed and the Lord miraculously opened doors. Through a series of incredible events, Chloe ended up moving to Taiwan for 11th and 12th grades. This unique opportunity was presented at the perfect time and Chloe had a wonderful experience during her time in Taiwan; I have also met some of my best and lifelong friends at the Morrison Academy. Her time provided us insights that will have an enduring impact on the children at Project Canaan.

After Chloe graduated from Morrison Academy, she moved to Canada for university—with her parental support system still a million miles away, but with Spencer a little closer in the U.S. Both Spencer and Chloe did really well, even as teenagers who were forced to make a lot of adult decisions early in life, but they were also raised by two pretty independent people and had a lot of life experiences that helped prepare them, at least a bit, for the real world.

Our concern for the children of Project Canaan is that while they are being raised in a healthy and happy environment, getting the best education money can buy, they are still living on an island—in a "bubble," as some people would say. They will need more help navigating the real world than Spencer and Chloe did. This is not a new phenomenon; in fact, there are many children in the west who were raised by very protective parents and failed miserably when they left for university. I remember a friend telling us that he and his wife hadn't believed in their children sleeping over in other people's houses (not an uncommon protection practice), so when their son left for university, it was the first time he had ever slept outside his parents' home without them. That alone put unusual stress on the young teen trying to figure out life without mom and dad.

How will we prepare our Swazi children for life in Eswatini when they have been brought up so differently than anyone else in the country? They have been raised as Swazi children, but with significant influence from other cultures. I have been thinking about this a lot since the day that Joshua arrived and people ask me about it all the time because there are so many horror stories of children "aging out" of alternative care facilities and failing miserably at life. Those teenagers aren't prepared for the real world, they don't have a support system in place, and honestly, 18-year-old people don't even have fully developed brains, yet!

I have been praying about it, speaking with many other homes who have been doing this for a long time and have experienced the heartache of their young adults suffering once they leave the home. No one seems to have "cracked the nut" of how to have these special children move on to the next phase of life in a healthy manner.

While I am comforted knowing that our oldest children are only 9 as I type this, I'm reminded that we "only have nine more years to go." We need to start being more proactive and intentional about building a program to bridge the 18 to 21-year-old gap, including how to find a job, a place to live, and perhaps more importantly, a way to live. We will call this project "The Bridge" and are currently looking for a few good minds to help us think this through.

The Christian Alliance for Orphans (CAFO) focuses on five areas for their children who are "aging out" of the system in which they are being raised. These are the five areas that we also want to help our children as they cross the bridge to adulthood. They include:

1. Life skills training

2. Spiritual care and mentoring

3. Transitional housing

4. Career development

5. Church and community support networks

There is a home in El Salvador that has what they call a "Transitional Care Home." That is a place specifically designed for their children to call home up to the age of 22 years, as they complete their post-secondary education, enter the workforce, etc. This is something that we will need to think through as well.

One day, while I was praying about the development of this plan, I had an interesting thought. There is a phenomenon that is not new, but might be new to you, called "Third Culture Kids (TCK)." This is a concept that was introduced to us through the Morrison Academy. Let me use Chloe as an example. Chloe grew up in Canada as a Canadian, was raised by Canadian parents, and got a Canadian education (well, except for her time in the U.S.). Then, she moved to Eswatini and eventually on to Taiwan to go to Morrison Academy. The other students in that school either came from Taiwanese homes, parents, or families or from American homes, parents, or families. Most of the American kids' parents were missionaries in Asia, so perhaps they hadn't lived much in the U.S., but would identify themselves as Americans because they had American passports. When these students, teachers, and families all united at Morrison Academy, they then created their own culture by mixing and blending their own cultures and cultural differences. This is what is called the "third culture." There is much more to this concept, and some might be frustrated by my simplification of it, but I hope they will forgive me as I try to keep this simple. Here is a summary from Wikipedia that explains some of the benefits and challenges that TCKs experience:

Benefits:

- TCKs have an understanding that there is more than one way to look at situations that they are exposed to or experience. This can also be a challenge, however, when TCKs return to a culture that is homogenous in their belief system, as an expanded worldview is perceived as offensive or useless.

- Interpersonal sensitivity: Increased exposure to a variety of perceptions and lifestyles allow TCKs to monitor their emotion, and register societal norms and cues more adeptly, so as to produce higher sensitivity to other cultures and ways of life.

- Cross-cultural competence or cultural intelligence: the capacity to function effectively across national, ethnic, and organizational cultures.

- TCKs have been found to have higher levels of general adjustment as opposed to mono-cultural children. Cultural adaptability is also a benefit, although may also come as a challenge that results from a lack of cultural balance.

Challenges:

- Confused loyalties: Third culture kids can experience a lot of confusion with politics and values. This is especially the case when moving from collectivist to individualist cultures, or vice versa, as the values within each culture are different from the other. This issue is also related to the identity crisis, on a cultural level, not being able to feel a sense of oneness with any one nationality or culture. Oftentimes, TCKs cannot answer the question: "Where is home?"

- Difficulties with adjusting to adult life: the mixture of influences from the various cultures that the individual has lived can create challenges in developing an identity as well as with a sense of belonging. Feelings of rootlessness and restlessness can make the transition to adulthood a challenging period for TCKs.

The issue of identity comes into play with TCKs in a very unique way. We want to be prepared to leverage the benefits of being a TCK while addressing some of the challenges that they might uniquely experience. Morrison Academy did a wonderful job at preparing their students throughout their senior year for life as a TCK after high school. They gave tangible examples of how they are different from other people, practical tools and life skills that are unique to TCKs, and encouraged them to embrace their uniqueness. We hope to engage experts in this area to help us when the time comes.

Our eldest children are in third grade right now, but even now we can start to identify the kids who are good at math or love to play the guitar or like to help out in the kitchen. By the time they are in seventh grade, we want to be intentional in assessing children's aptitudes and skills. Later in high school, we want to start a mentor program where local and foreign volunteers could work alongside the students to start thinking about the future, helping them dream, plan and prepare for life after high school. Some students will want to go on to university, others will get trades training either on Project Canaan or elsewhere, and some may just want to get a job. We want to help each child be the very best that they can be, given the unique upbringing they have experienced. Building "The Bridge" that will take our children beyond high school and into the world will be a critical next step for us to think through and plan well. We will need to create an endowment soon that can help provide the resources for our children to cross the bridge well and succeed. If we can "crack this nut," we could become a training center for other alternative care facilities around the world. Our children could even become experts in the field and travel the world helping children in other homes "age out" well.

Wouldn't that be amazing?

CHAPTER TWELVE

A Paradigm Shift in My Thinking

It was early August 2020, when I received a call about a newborn baby who had just been found in the forest, still bloody from birth, umbilical cord attached, but crudely torn away from her mother's womb.

When I reached the hospital, the social worker told me that she had given the child a name, because she felt very strongly about doing so. (Often they leave the naming to us.) She told me that this baby would be called Usiphile Favor (pronounced Ooh-see-pee-lay). Usiphile means "He has sent us" in the siSwati language, so her name means "He has sent us favor."

I was writing an update to our monthly child sponsorship supporters and decided to tell them about baby Favor and add a piece of encouraging scripture. I went to *Biblegateway.com* and typed in "favor." Isaiah 61 immediately popped up, which was interesting, because just that morning I had read Isaiah 61 in my daily scripture reading. The headline read "The Year of the Lord's Favor:"

"The Spirit of the Sovereign LORD is on me, because the LORD has anointed me to preach good news to the poor. He has sent me to bind up the brokenhearted, to proclaim freedom for the captives and release from darkness the prisoners, to proclaim the year of the LORD's favor and the day of vengeance of our God, to comfort all who mourn, and provide for those who grieve in Zion-- to bestow on them a crown of beauty instead of ashes, the oil of gladness instead of mourning, and a garment of praise instead of a spirit of despair. They will be called oaks of righteousness, a planting of the LORD for the display of his splendor" Isaiah 61:1-3.

It was at that moment that I had a paradigm shift. We were deep into the first five months of Covid-19, which was wreaking havoc all over the world and no less so in the Kingdom of Eswatini. When we first had to send most of our workers home due to the countrywide lockdown, I wept in my house, because I believed that I wouldn't ever see many of these workers again. They were all leaving the farm with their heads low, shoulders bent, and a fear of death that I have not seen on a corporate level before. I felt it and was already mourning. I was making plans of what to do when my senior staff at our children's campus were called home to look after their own children as their children's caregivers (mother or grandmother) succumbed to the deadly virus.

Who would we hire to care for our children? New cases and deaths were rising rapidly in the U.S. and in our neighbor, South Africa, and I was afraid. The borders had been closed for many months and I was captive—we were captive, like prisoners who had nowhere to go and could not escape. When the first lockdown was released a bit, some of our more essential workers could come back to work and I was relieved, but we were still stuck.

Over the months. I continued my time of mourning. I mourned that we could not be together as a family in Cape Town to celebrate Chloe's graduation from university and then celebrate her 24th birthday in Eswatini. I mourned that we couldn't be with Spencer when he proposed marriage to his longtime girlfriend, Jane (whom he met on a *Heart for Africa* trip in Eswatini, I might add). I then moved on to mourn that we couldn't go to Canada for Chloe's graduation or see Ian's parents or celebrate Spencer's 26th birthday in Chicago. In hindsight, there was a lot of self-pity in which I allowed myself to engage from time to time, but only for a day. I thought I was well disciplined in that area. (Perhaps not.)

On that day in August, it all changed for me—all because the Lord sent us a baby named "He is sending us favor" and then I read Isaiah 61 (for the second time that day) and realized that this is the year of the Lord's favor. What on earth had I been thinking? I started to look around me and saw all that He has been doing during this terrible year of Covid-19. Rather than thinking about the memes on Facebook that describe the year as terrible, or "wishing my mother really could smack me into next year!" or my favorite one that read, "2020 the Movie. Written by Stephen King. Directed by Quinton Tarantino. Music by Yoyo Ma." I thought that was hilarious and it described how I had been feeling.

As I read Isaiah 61, it jumped off the page like scripture had not done before: I am to proclaim the good news to the poor (not just lament in bad news, over and over)! I am to be (myself) released from the darkness of prison and to comfort those who mourn, but not to mourn that which has not died.

"Bestow on them a crown of beauty instead of ashes, the oil of gladness instead of mourning and a garment of praise instead of a spirit of despair" (verse 3).

I was living in a state of mourning with a heavy dose of the spirit of despair, but why? It was because the whole world was talking about Covid-19: the cases, the deaths, the economic impact, the uncertainty, and even hopelessness.

It was like a giant curtain was pulled back on that day and I looked at my world differently. This was the year of the Lord's favor for *Heart for Africa* and Project Canaan. We had the funds to start building Emseni 6 for our older boys and O2, our huge, two-story recreation center, and our dining hall. We had the funds to build two-story classrooms for two each the third and fourth grades. We had hired a full-time farm manager, who was maximizing the utilization of our irrigated fields, producing a bountiful harvest for consumption and for sale. He was able to increase employment opportunities when most companies were laying people off or closing their doors. Our greenhouse was flourishing with fresh produce that went straight from farm to table, providing healthy food for our children at a reduced price from what we would pay in town. We were given a significant amount of money from a man in Canada, of whom we had never heard or even received a donation in the past, and that allowed us to expand our dairy. Not only did we not know him, but he had passed away and left these funds for *Heart for Africa* in his will. They were just what we needed to get Phase One of the project moving forward so that we could expand the capacity for more dairy cattle—which meant more milk production, which meant more income generation. The water is flowing freely down the mountain and our dams are full. With water security we were able to expand our irrigated fields by an additional 17 acres, allowing us to grow alfalfa to feed our dairy herd. All of this was happening right in front of my eyes during the time of Covid-19.

This year of the Lord's favor also included funding to import a new water filtration system from Israel that produces 1,100 gallons of clean drinking water per hour to the entire property, ensuring that no deadly waterborne illnesses are present. (We had outgrown our original system.) We were given funding to create an intensive goat-breeding program, which included 10 acres of fenced area, complete with structures for breeding, birthing, and treatment (including a foot bath). We even received the funds to build an African-style fire station (made from two 20-ft containers) that will house large portable water tanks that can be lowered into trucks to help us fight fires with water. (What a novel thought.)

Another area of mourning for me had been what was happening at our 30 church partners and their feeding programs. Most of our churches only feed the children on Saturday and Sunday because most children were able to get food at school feeding programs from Monday-Thursday. (Remember schools close early on Friday, so that they don't have to feed the kids.) Due to Covid-19, the schools were closed, with hopes to reopen in 2021, and the children were at home, starving. Our dear friends and partner, *Feed My Starving Children*, depend completely upon volunteers to hand pack the MannaPack™ that they ship to us to feed the children; those packing sites were closed immediately when Covid-19 hit the U.S. Where would we get food when the children needed it more than ever?

Voila! The Lord provided more food! Our volunteer nurse, Rebekah Rutledge, told us about an organization called *Gleanings for the Hungry* in California and she reached out to them to see if they could help. Within a few weeks, they had a 40-ft container of dried beans and dried soup mix (filled with pasta, rice, and dried vegetables of all kinds) on a shipping container to Eswatini, with another one on route only three months later. Not only was the second container filled with 44,000+ pounds of dried food, we were able to add boxes of special treats for our long-term volunteers living in Eswatini, who also couldn't leave the country or go home to visit family, stock up on favorite foods or necessities. Then we heard about an organization in British Columbia, Canada, called *The Gleaners*, which is a similar organization to *Gleanings for the Hungry*, and they agreed to partner with us and send a 40-ft container of dried vegetables and dried apple chips. The Lord was still providing food while *Feed My Starving Children* worked to get their MannaPack™ packed by machine.

The Lord was providing favor through food and we started approaching our churches about what it would take to start feeding the children seven days a week. While funding prospects from churches and organizations in the U.S. and Canada came to a grinding halt in March when churches closed, we had an individual donor who provided the funds for us to build our first permanent cooking and storage structure with our first church partner in August 2020—the same month my paradigm shift happened.

I have listed many of the projects with which the Lord has shown us great favor over the past few months, but I would remiss to not mention the fact that our children's campuses have been the healthiest they have ever been. Yes, it could be because we are washing our hands more and sanitizing at every turn, and it could also be that we have been on lockdown, not allowing anyone to enter the campus unless they are absolutely essential (staff, appliance repair, food delivery) and always wearing a mask; it is the law to do so. Our children are not wearing masks, but they are not leaving the property or being exposed to others who do.

We also haven't even had the seasonal flu go through our staff and children and we *always* get the flu, no matter how hard we try to keep it at bay. We have had a lot of sicknesses at the Khutsala Artisans shop and the El Rofi Medical clinic has been inundated with sick people with flu-like (or Covid-19-like) symptoms, but testing is very limited here, so Nurse Anthony sends them home to self-isolate for 14 days. We have been protected and every staff member has seen that protection and is in awe of the health that we are experiencing.

All of the things I have reported above were happening during my time of mourning and despair. *Can you imagine?* Needless to say, I have repented. Each and every day I now get up and claim this the year of the Lord's favor. In fact, having read this whole book and the many stories of God's repeated provision, wouldn't you agree that the favor of the Lord has been with us from the very beginning?

The rest of Isaiah 61 says this,

"They will rebuild the ancient ruins and restore the places long devastated;

they will renew the ruined cities that have been devastated for generations.

Aliens will shepherd your flocks; foreigners will work your fields and vineyards.

And you will be called priests of the LORD, you will be named ministers of our God.

You will feed on the wealth of nations, and in their riches you will boast. Instead of their shame my people will receive a double portion, and instead of disgrace they will rejoice in their inheritance;

and so they will inherit a double portion in their land, and everlasting joy will be theirs.

'For I, the LORD, love justice; I hate robbery and iniquity.

In my faithfulness I will reward them and make an everlasting covenant with them.

Their descendants will be known among the nations and their offspring among the peoples. All who see them will acknowledge that they are a people the LORD has blessed.'

I delight greatly in the LORD; my soul rejoices in my God.

For he has clothed me with garments of salvation and arrayed me in a robe of righteousness, as a bridegroom adorns his head like a priest,

and as a bride adorns herself with her jewels.

For as the soil makes the sprout come up and a garden causes seeds to grow,

so the Sovereign LORD will make righteousness

and praise spring up before all nations."

Not everything has been perfect during this time of favor, but we have chosen to (tried to) give thanks in all things. Sometimes that's harder to do than others.

One day in June, we noticed that our Doberman, Max, had a large lump on his chest, and another one that seemed to have appeared out of nowhere under his front arm. One was the size of a lemon and the other the size of a grapefruit. We drove an hour to the veterinarian and he told us that it was most likely cancer, but with the borders closed, there was no way to send him for tests in South Africa; they couldn't be done in Eswatini.

We were devastated. Max came to live with us as a small puppy only weeks after we first moved to Swaziland in 2012, and he was not only the best dog ever, but he was Ian's dog, the alpha of the pack and our protector. Swazis were afraid of this giant and perfect specimen of a Doberman and that ultimately helped with our protection and the protection of our property at night. Max (and the others) would be locked up during the day and was let out to roam our personal property, within the confines of our electric fencing, to keep us all safe from intruders.

After the lumps were discovered, Max had a few good weeks and then his health started to decline. He was slower to move, stopped eating, and then, started to self-isolate away from the other dogs. Not long afterward, we made the heartbreaking decision to take him back to the vet and have to be euthanized. We knew that the vet would give him the injection in the back of Ian's truck and we would have to drive our dead dog back to the farm to be buried. We tried to mentally prepare for that awful hour.

We arrived at the vet a few minutes before our appointment. We sat on the side of the road and I put on some Christian music from Ian's phone.

The song that played was unfamiliar to us, but it was a gift from the Lord at that moment. It is called *The Blessing* and was the live version performed by Kari Jobe, Codey Carnes, and the Elevation Worship. It is a classical benediction composition, based on *Numbers 6:24-26* and written by John Rutter. The song starts very sweetly with the words, "The Lord bless you. And keep you. Make His face shine upon you. And be gracious to you. The Lord turn His Face toward you. And give you peace." Those words were sung over and over and I felt the presence of the Lord wash over me as tears washed down my face. What a beautiful song to play "randomly" on our playlist as we waited to say goodbye to our dear friend and family member. Then, the song changed. It got more intense and they started singing "May *His favor* be upon you. And a thousand generations. Your family and your children. And their children and their children. May His favor be upon you. And a thousand generations. And your family and your children. And their children and their children and their children …"

I wept. May His favor be upon us and our children and their children? What an incredible blessing this was and oh, how I wish I had seen His favor that day, but I knew He was with us. As I type these words, I am filled to overflowing with the promise that not only Spencer and Chloe, but also the children who are being raised at Project Canaan, are our children and they *do* have His favor on them and so will their children and their children. The curses have been broken.

"Instead of shame they will receive a double portion and instead of disgrace they will rejoice in their inheritance. … Their children will be known among nations and all who see them will acknowledge that they are a people the Lord has blessed. For as the soil makes sprout to come

up and a garden causes seeds to grow, so the Sovereign Lord will make righteousness and praise spring up before all nations." (Isaiah 61, again, paraphrased).

As Covid-19 continues to cause havoc around the world, it is hard to not wonder what the future looks like for this tiny Kingdom. While we do not have the death rates that other countries are experiencing, it is widely agreed that poverty, leading to starvation and other illnesses, is likely to kill more people than the virus itself. There was an article in the newspaper recently with a headline that read *"Teenage Pregnancy 'National Disaster'"* and it went on to talk about the vast number of teenagers who are getting pregnant while schools are closed: adults are home due to unemployment and the victim pool of the rape culture is ripe and accessible. Female teachers are often responsible for noticing if a young female student becomes withdrawn, starts behaving differently, or sees her small belly starting to grow; and, it is female teachers who often become the recipient of the rape report.

There was another article in the newspaper where a Regional Administrator (also a prominent Chief) was asking for laws to be changed so that pregnant girls could attend school and take their exams while pregnant when schools reopen. Current laws force pregnant girls to drop out of school. The Chief stated that it was well known that, because the schools are closed due to Covid-19 and most families ran out of food in March, there are many students who are not getting a meal at the closed school or at home. Hunger and lockdown made life difficult for people to escape abuse and human temptations, thereby causing unwanted pregnancies. Our school year runs from the end of January to the end of November, but schools closed in March due to the virus and they are not expected to reopen until 2021. Even our pastors are calling us to report that many of the girls in their communities are being attacked, mostly at home by a known relative with whom the girls live. They are not safe at home and there is nowhere else for them to go.

While we fear that a huge wave of babies will be coming our way in early 2021, we are also praying that the suicide rate of these young girls does not start to spike, along with the unnecessary deaths due to attempted home abortion. I once read that 90 percent of all female deaths in the main government hospital were due to botched home abortions. With Covid-19, people are avoiding the hospitals like the plague—or should I say: they are avoiding them to avoid the plague. My heart continues to hurt for the girls and women of Africa and especially Eswatini, but I know the Lord is here and I pray that He hears their cries.

One good piece of news is that Eswatini passed a Sexual Offense & Domestic Violence law in August 2019 (better late than never), which actually makes it illegal to beat or rape your wife and it seems to be an easier legal charge to make for the rape of a minor, rather than invoking the Child Protection Act of 2012. Since last August, thousands of girls and have come forward, most of them minors, and brought charges against men for sexual assault and ongoing sexual abuse. There is an article in the paper *every day*, calling out men by name for their crimes. This is all good news. While it will take time for the message to be heard by all Swazis, it may never be embraced by the older generation and "deep Swazis," who believe that women are property and daughters, nieces, and granddaughters are there for the taking.

I remember the first time I heard about "first fruits" here in Eswatini. I was riding in a long car ride with one of my children's campus supervisors, from whom I always learn a lot about Swazi culture. It seems every time we get in the car together, another layer of the onion is peeled back from Swazi culture and I am exposed to new information that I couldn't dream up. She asked me if I knew the story in the Bible about giving the first fruits to the Lord. Of course I did. While I'm not a Bible scholar, nor have I been very disciplined at scripture memorization, I remembered that we are to bring the first fruits of our harvest to the Lord. *Exodus 23:19* and *Numbers 18:13* (I looked those up!) Ian and I have been very intentional about giving away a tenth of our first maize crop to families in need, so yes, I understood the concept. She explained that some Swazi families believe that when the maize is ready to be harvested, the father of the homestead is the one to go and taste it first to see if it is sweet. She went on to explain that they also believe the same is true of their daughters—the father is to taste the "fruit" first to see if it is sweet before any other boy or man touches his daughter.

Serving in another culture can be very challenging; there are days when it is really hard for me not to judge what I am being told and to keep an open mind. Some days, it is really difficult for me to not slam on the breaks, pull the car over, and turn my head with my jaw dropped open and say, "Are you freaking kidding me?" (I realize I'm not hiding my judgment well at all.) To understand what some of our children have experienced and, especially, to understand the perspective and possible experiences that our staff has encountered or endured, we must be intentional in creating a space of quiet to listen, a space of openness to understand, and a space of love for healing to begin.

While Eswatini is made up of one tribe and one language, there are different families (like clans) who have very different traditions, some that are not known outside that family name and others that are well known. Some of the traditions include human sacrifice as a part of their worship service and others include dietary restrictions. Some are steeped in tradition, darkness, and ancestral worship and others are less sinister. For example, everyone knows that a Dlamini (popular name in siSwati—in fact, the King's surname) can't eat lamb or they will go mad. The Matsenjwa family doesn't eat goat for the same reasons. This all could have started with someone's personal preference ("Gogo Dlamini didn't like lamb meat, so she told everyone not to eat it or they would go mad." Or maybe "Gogo Matsenjwa had a nervous breakdown after eating goat one night and the family decided to stay away from that meat thenceforth.")

We all have those things in our families, traditions whose origin we may not even know, but hopefully, they are not harmful to others and are not demonic in nature. The Jericho sect of the Zionist Church doesn't eat pork because, in the Bible, the demons were sent into pigs and they ran over the cliff and drowned in the water below, so they believe that pigs are demonic. We are trying to weed out the harmful and demonic practices, leaving them at the gate before entering, and embrace the good and healthy parts of Swazi culture and history. The sexual assault and "rape culture" that is prevalent here seems to cross all families, clans, religious sects, and denominations. It is a spirit that is not welcome on Project Canaan and we pray daily for protection from that evil.

Just as I needed a paradigm shift in my thinking during this year of confusion, fear, and uncertainty, to see this as a year of blessing and favor, I also needed a paradigm shift in my thinking and approach to serving Swazis in their own culture. It is hard to not think that our way is the best way or even the right way, but that is rarely true. One thing I learned many years ago while hearing an African pastor preach on culture versus the gospel was this: As Christians, we must be very gracious and open to the culture in which we are working, but when culture clashes with the gospel, the gospel must trump. We do things the way we do them because of the way we were raised, the education we were given (or not given), and the way we have seen things done, but it doesn't mean that we are right and they are wrong. In the case of child rape and domestic violence, the scriptures say that those are wrong, so the Bible wins over popular cultural norms here.

Here is an example of the opposite of this that might make you smile— and will surely make my Swazi friends laugh out loud. Swazis make something called "emasi" and they *love it*! In fact, it would be considered a favorite food to many. What is "emasi?" For my western friends, think about that time that you went away on holiday and left milk in the fridge. When you came back and smelled it, you started to pour it down the sink and heard the "glunk, glunk, glunk" of the solid, sour milk. That's emasi—well, almost. Emasi is made by taking unpasteurized milk, covering it, and leaving it outside in a warm place for three or four days until it is thick and chunky. Then you put it in a bowl, serve with a spoon, and every Swazi in the house is happy (except those who are allergic to dairy product—so perhaps their children won't eat emasi in the future because it made their mom or dad sick and that is how family traditions begin or change). When I first started working on the menu plan for our children and staff, I met with my senior people and asked what would typically be on a Swazi menu. The list was short and included maize, spinach, beetroot, and butternut squash. Lettuce and tomato would be included if there was money to grow or buy them, and of course, emasi.

I was all for the first six items, but there was no way I was having sour milk made out of perfectly good fresh cow's milk and I most certainly was not serving it to my children and staff. Well, never say never. Emasi is a part of Swazi culture that is not harmful; it's comfort food and everyone loves it. Just because I don't love it, it doesn't mean it should be left off the menu.

We have had a lifetime of learning since we started serving in Africa almost 20 years ago. Back in the early days, we used to say that the learning curve was vertical, but I'm not sure that it has changed much in all those years. To use a current expression, we haven't seen a "flattening of the curve" of learning, but instead try to embrace every day as a new adventure with something new to learn. Through learning, we have a few new things to teach. I would say that one of the most important lessons we have learned is to listen more, speak less, and leave space in the conversation for our African brothers and sisters to talk. We tend to be quick to speak, make decisions, and move on to the next thing. That is not how things are done here. Somewhere between our rush to move forward and the Swazis' desire to keep things as they are, there is the place where we must meet to get buy-in and achieve mutual success. There are still so many things that we don't know—and we don't even know what we don't know. Nor do we know what the people with whom we are working don't know. (That was a tongue twister!) So, we must be intentional in our willingness to look for new ways of doing things, consider old ways of doing things (avoid learning everything the hard way), and pray for the Lord's direction in all things. It's a paradigm shift in thinking.

In what area of your life do you need a paradigm shift today?

As I sit overlooking the farm, seeing the Parmalat truck pick up milk from the dairy, watching the goats graze, seeing men and women harvesting vegetables in the fields, and hearing the voices of children wafting up over the hill, I am overwhelmed by a sense of peace and gratitude for having been invited into this story.

Many people have commented over the years that if Ian and I had not said "yes" to this calling, all the children who have been rescued and living on Project Canaan would be dead. We disagree completely. If Ian and I had said "no," I believe that these children would still be alive because it is the Lord who numbers our days. Their homes would look different, the schools would look different, and systems and approaches would be different, but the children would be alive and a part of His plan for the future.

The truth is that our family would have missed the blessing of being able to be a part of their rescue, rehabilitation, and redemption. Ian would have missed the opportunity to learn about dairy cows and how to start an aquaponics project; he would never have known how to build a dam to capture rainwater or the realities of drought and the importance of water security. Spencer and Chloe would have lived their lives in Ontario, venturing to holiday resorts from time to time, with little to no understanding of other cultures, customs that were unlike their own, or the depth of global poverty. They would have missed the opportunity to be a part of feeding starving children, rescuing abandoned babies, creating employment, and helping educate a generation of African children. I would never have known the bittersweet joy of being present at the birth of a baby to a 13-year-old girl or been able to wipe the tears of an old gogo, who was so happy that her grandson would be saved from starvation with hope on his horizon.

We all would have missed seeing the hand of God at work, day in and day out. We would have missed seeing miracles and wonders, redemption through pain, and hope through salvation. What a tragic loss that would have been for all of us; I shudder at the thought.

Have you ever wondered if you have missed an opportunity to help someone in need? Do you remember the time that you were invited into someone's story (aka asked to help another person), but were too busy, distracted, or scared to help? I remember Oprah Winfrey being asked by a guest what the opposite of love is. She answered "hate." The guest replied, "No, the opposite of love is indifference."

That struck me like an arrow to my heart. Was I indifferent to the world around me? Who was I supposed to not be indifferent about? Family? Neighbors? Starving children in Africa? I never thought of myself as a person who hated other people, but was I indifferent to other people (and their problems)? This "love and hate" question was asked in the very early days of my personal transformation and I spent a lot of time thinking about it. Time, prayer, reading, education, and longing to love others led first to a change in my heart, then next, was me having a heart for Africa. The blindfold of indifference was torn from my eyes, forcing me to see the truth about injustice around the world. My heart was ripped open by the oppression that I witnessed, which was killing the hearts and souls of a generation of Africans.

It was the hopelessness that truly shattered me. I didn't know such a thing existed until I first came to Africa. How could someone dump a newborn baby in a pit latrine? *Hopelessness.* How could a young girl repeatedly have unwanted sex with an old man? *Hopelessness.* How could a mother be relieved to give away her newborn baby to strangers? *Hopelessness.*

One day, I decided to no longer be indifferent to hopelessness and that decision changed my life. Will you make that decision today, too? Will you join us in bringing real hope to the next generation of leaders in Eswatini? It takes a very large village to raise a lot of children, but will you join us in helping our children, to paraphrase Mahatma Ghandi "be the change we want to see in the world?"

The time for indifference is over.

Hope is alive and hope lives at Project Canaan.

"For I know the plans I have for you," declares the LORD, "plans to prosper you and not to harm you, plans to give you hope and a future. Then you will call upon me and come and pray to me, and I will listen to you. You will seek me and find me when you seek me with all your heart" Jeremiah 29:11.

A Letter to Our Children

To our dear children,

By the time you read this letter, you will likely be excelling in whatever area of life the Lord has perfectly planned for you. We will never forget the day you arrived because that was a day that changed our lives and yours. We may never know specifically why God brought you to this big Project Canaan family, but we always knew that His plans are perfect and you were a perfect addition to our family.

We believe that the Lord called us to be a mother (make) and father (babe), and for Spencer to be a big brother and Chloe to be a big sister to every Swazi child the Lord placed with us. We hope that you will always know that you were chosen and loved by your heavenly Father by how you were loved by us. Babe tried to be a good father who cares for and provides for his children, teaching them the importance of hard work, honesty and integrity. Make tried to be a good mother by showing love, discipline, and the importance of always telling the truth.

No one knows how many days we have on earth, but we all know that our days are numbered and we all know that one day we will die. It's like the old expression, "The only two things for sure in life are death and taxes." My dad loved that one. I could die before I finish this letter (maybe I should have written it first!), but hopefully, I will live for many more years to be able to impart these pearls of wisdom, in person; however, would be remiss to have more than 300 children and not leave them all with a few thoughts in writing. These are in no particular order, as Ian and I think they are all important:

- *You were chosen, by God, to be put in this family for a reason and a purpose that is unique only to you. Seek that purpose with all your heart, giving thanks for whatever life's circumstances have been given to you. Like Joseph from the Bible, you just never know what is in store in the future. You might just save a nation.*

- *You are responsible for making good choices or bad choices. You are responsible for your mood. Don't blame someone else for something for which you are responsible.*

- *Choose your friends wisely, as they have a huge impact on whether you make good choices or bad choices (and they also can influence your mood). If you want to see how people perceive you, look around at the friends with whom you surround yourselves because they are a reflection of you. My father used to say, "Fish will always swim toward water," which means, people will always look for people who are like themselves.*

- *Jesus is watching over you and wants to guide and direct you. He is not trying to trick you into making the wrong choice. He really does want the very best for you and will give you the desires of your heart if you are walking with Him. I promise you, it works! Look at us living on a mountaintop in Africa, serving Him. I couldn't have asked for anything better.*

- *Integrity—do what you say you are going to do, always, or don't say you can or will do it. It is really important that people know that you are a person who can be trusted.*

- *Look out for the little ones. When Ian worked at his first job as a busboy at the Ottawa Civic Hospital, there was a guy who worked in the kitchen who was a very simple man. One day, he walked up to Ian and randomly said, "We need to look out for the little ones." And he walked away. That stuck with Ian his whole life. It is a universal truth that little ones are innocent and must be protected.*

- *Be sure to rest one day of the week. Ian and I were taught that practice as children and our parents always rested on Sunday after church. It was boring as kids because everyone had to take a nap, but as adults, you will be really happy to have enjoyed a Sunday afternoon nap. If your employment requires you to work on Sunday, then choose another day to be your Sabbath and do it faithfully. This is one of the Ten Commandments and is as important as "Do not murder" (Exodus 20:8-11).*

- *When you are making money at a job, whether you are making a little money or a lot, tithe first (10 percent to the Lord), save next, spend last. We believe that everything we have comes from the Lord. It is all His and we are only stewards of what He has given us. Ten percent is the least we should give. Be sure to tithe and also gift generously.*

- *Make your own decisions; don't let someone else make decisions for you. My mom used to say, "Don't get in the backseat with a boy and then try to decide to say 'no.' Make the decision **not** to get in the backseat. That's an easier choice."*

- *I used to whine to my mom and say "That's not fair," to which she always responded, "Janine, life isn't fair." While I didn't like that answer much, it was truth. "Justice may not be fair, but God is a just God." Read Isaiah 30:18.*

- *Truth is truth, wherever it may be found. If a homeless person on the side of the road speaks the truth to you, it is no less true than if it comes from the Holy Scriptures. Believe in and search for absolute truths.*

- *If you want it to be easy, it has to be hard. Laying a foundation for anything takes time and patience. You'll know what we mean when you encounter this.*

- *Try to only learn hard lessons once, and if possible, learn them from watching a friend make mistakes. Learn from their mistake, so you can cross that one off your list.*

- *Be sure to teach your children to be thankful in all things, the good and the bad. A thankful spirit can heal hurt, mend relationships and keep your body and mind healthy. Read James 1:2-4*

- *When you want to ask for something (i.e. a favor, a job, something from your parents), do your homework or research first. Think about how that person may respond, including the answers to any questions or reservations that might be given back to you. A Maxwell family motto was always "Make it an easy 'yes.'" Don't be afraid to ask for what you want—you've already got "no."*

- *Ian and I will celebrate 30 years of marriage on October 5, 2021. Here is a piece of marriage advice that has served us well, especially in the early days: if you are trying to decide what to have for dinner, what movie to watch, or what activity to do on the weekend and you both have a different opinion, there is a way to be fair to each other. The easiest way is to submit to the other person because you want your spouse to be happy. If that isn't where you are emotionally, then try this: on a scale of one to 10 (one being low, 10 being high), each of you must say how important it is to eat that food or see that movie. You have to be **honest** (no cheating allowed!). If I really desired pizza for dinner, I might say "nine or 10. If Ian really wanted KFC for dinner, he might say "eight," but my nine or 10 is higher, so we would have pizza. After a few years of this, you should move past the number system and just know when your spouse wants to see an action movie rather than a love story. Remember, no cheating.*

- *When mama's happy, everybody's happy. Words to live by.*

- *Do everything you do with excellence.*

- *The Bible tells us to love one another and we must actively do that in our daily lives, but be careful about using the word "love" with a boyfriend or girlfriend. Saying "I love you" to a person with whom you are in a romantic relationship should be reserved for a time when you are ready to make a long-term commitment of marriage to that person.*

- *There will always be someone richer than you.*

- *You're going to make people mad no matter what you do in life, so at least, do something that matters.*

- *Do not put anything in writing that you do not want to be read in court. That includes text messages, social media, email, or handwritten notes—not a love letter, not a threat, **nothing**.*

- ***Remember you are loved!***

I think this letter could go on and on, but really, if you just read the book of Proverbs, you will get all of the above and more. Please know that we are proud of you, we love you, and we pray all of God's richest blessings on your lives.

Lots of love,

Mom and Dad

HELP US FIGHT HUNGER

For more information or to get involved, go to:
www.heartforafrica.org/hunger

Bringing HOPE to Eswatini, Africa

HELP US CARE FOR ORPHANS

For more information or to get involved, go to:
www.heartforafrica.org/orphans

Bringing HOPE to Eswatini, Africa

HELP US DECREASE POVERTY

For more information or to get involved, go to:
www.heartforafrica.org/poverty

or scan code

Bringing HOPE to Eswatini, Africa

HELP US PROVIDE EDUCATION

For more information or to get involved, go to:
www.heartforafrica.org/education

Bringing HOPE to Eswatini, Africa

Made in the USA
Monee, IL
02 June 2021